▼

from
JUNG
to
JESUS

▼

Myth and Consciousness in the New Testament

GERALD H. SLUSSER

John Knox Press
ATLANTA

Library of Congress Cataloging-in-Publication Data

Slusser, Gerald H.
    From Jung to Jesus.

    Bibliography: p.
    Includes index.
    1. Jesus Christ—Psychology.   2. Bible.   N.T.
Gospels—Criticism, interpretation, etc.   3. Jung,
C. G. (Carl Gustav), 1875-1961.   4. Campbell, Joseph,
1904-   5. Heroes—Religious aspects.   I. Title.
BT590.P9S58   1986   232   85-45792
ISBN 0-8042-1111-6

Appreciation

Thanks and immense intellectual and inspirational indebtedness are due to the many scholars whose names are found in the Notes and without whose efforts this work would have been impossible. Personal thanks are due to several professional friends and colleagues who read various portions of the manuscript and made very helpful suggestions: Professor Lionel Whiston, my colleague at Eden Seminary; Professors Joanmarie Smith and Gloria Durka; Pastor Nico Ter Linden of Amsterdam; and two Eden students, Patrice and Sloan Bittner-Humphreys, who read and proofed the entire manuscript. I am immensely grateful to the Reverend Janice Springer, who read the manuscript in draft copy and prepared the index, and to Marie Morgan, my very careful copyeditor. Personally, I owe the greatest thanks to my wife for her loving patience during the years of research that preoccupied me in preparing this work and for her excellent skill in typing the manuscript and lovingly pointing out those sentences that "just don't make sense." Much of whatever clarity this attempt to write about a complex topic may have attained is due to her skill as an editor.

Preface

I will write about two matters in this preface: first, inclusive language; and second, the nature of this book and its intended audience. It seems advisable to clarify these matters now so that you, the reader, will approach this book from an informed perspective.

Concerning inclusive language, it is my commitment and that of John Knox Press to abstain from all use of sexist language insofar as is consistent with good style and readability. In this time of increasing sensitivity to the formative capacity of language, care in the use of words is particularly important. In this book an issue of considerable importance is at stake because the study focuses on the archetypal Hero figure, especially as that figure was manifested in the Gospel stories of Jesus. It is a fundamental thesis of the book that the Hero archetype is of central importance to understanding human nature in a religious perspective; yet, the vast majority of Hero stories left to us through the processes of history are male figures. It is my conviction that even in a male figure such as Jesus, the lineaments of the human situation both for men and for women are clearly revealed. That is, the steps of the Hero journey are not radically different for men than for women. It was my desire to make this conviction clear in the book by the use of the term *Hero/ine* and many other duplex terms such as *s/he* and *his/her*. In the editorial process, however, it became clear that this style resulted in a text that was awkward and pedantic. Thus, the decision was made to delete most of these duplex expressions. I do want to reit-

erate here that the essential pattern revealed in the Hero story as I
have discussed it in this book seems applicable to the spiritual journey both of men and of women. The differences are undeniable,
but the broad pattern does seem to apply to all of us. I hope that
these comments will help the reader understand that this book is
not just about the male spiritual journey but the female journey as
well.

In this same regard arises the use of gender pronouns for God.
It is my conviction that no human gender language is properly applicable to God, who is beyond all human distinctions and the author of all. So it is incorrect to address God as either He or She, yet
God is both Fatherly and Motherly, i.e., possessing characteristics
we attribute to the best of humanity, whether male or female.
Nonetheless, the English language is limited in its provisions, and
applying the pronoun it to God is inappropriate. Thus, wherever
possible, I have avoided pronouns.

The second matter, the nature of the book and its intended audience, is of equal importance. The book is intended to be read by
persons who are interested in the problems of the meaning and
purpose of human life and destiny, and the very complex problems
presented by the contemporary dialogue between science and religion, East and West. My intention is to suggest some ways of thinking and some things to think about. I have not written a critical or
dogmatic theology; rather, I have tried to write a thought-provok-
ing work about ultimate issues. The book is not written for the critical and well-informed biblical or Jungian scholars, although they,
too, may find food for thought in the theses presented. Because the
central focus is the Gospel stories of Jesus, this book must deal with
biblical interpretation and, equally, with the philosophical issue of
knowledge, what it is and how we get it and how we discern truth
from error.

Professor Walter Wink's famous line that the historical-critical
method of Scripture study is bankrupt may or may not be an over-
statement, but it is certain that contemporary Scripture study is in a
period of rapid transition, if not crisis. Beginning some forty years
ago, the German New Testament scholar Rudolf Bultmann advanced
the thesis that the Gospels contained much that was mythical and

thus much that required something other than historical interpretation. Bultmann decided that the ideas offered in the philosophy of Martin Heidegger could be of great value in determining the meaning of these difficult texts. His method became known in English as "demythologizing," as if one could translate mythic material into nonmythic ideas. I have a fundamental disagreement with this approach because I do not believe that ideas can be nonmythic (this matter will be addressed in some detail in the book's early chapters). Thus, I have chosen a way that is different from Bultmann's, a way that involves trying to understand the nature of human understanding as essentially mythic as well as rational and that uses the basic ideas of the psychology of C.G. Jung as the tool for interpreting myth.

It is my conviction that all human understanding is founded in myth and that archetypal symbols are the formative units of myth. These matters, which may sound rather technical, are explained in the early chapters. I do not intend by this position to fall into psychological reductionism, e.g., reducing all reality and history to myth, and in fact have tried to criticize this error as one of the problems in the modern worldview. In our human situation we always see through a glass darkly, as Saint Paul said, and the nature of God, reality, and our own souls is known only in images and metaphors. Certainly, religious matters cannot be reduced to psychological matters any more than one can say that God is simply "man writ large." In the final analysis all psychological matters are religious matters, not vice versa.

This book is written from an intentional Christian viewpoint but one that is informed about other world religions. It is my personal conviction that the life-death-resurrection of Jesus is the most important fact we have for understanding the meaning and destiny of human life. Yet this position does not seem to me to require us to reject or degrade the insights and parallels found in other religions and their Hero figures, such as Buddha or Krishna. Instead, I believe that we can see in these parallels the testimony that God has nowhere left people without saving knowledge and witnesses because the love of God is a universal love, including equally all peoples and all creation. We who stand within the Christian context, however, can learn very much from these other testimonies to the love and the presence of God and how they may be known. Finally, especially for those who have made some study of Jung, the question of the accuracy of my interpretation of Jung will arise. It is clear that even within the relatively close community of Jungian analysts there is disagreement about what Jung really said. Some, such as James Hillman, might be called revisionists; others, such as Erich Neumann, seem to be much closer to Jung's original thought. I make no effort to enter into, much less to address, these differences. My work is different: it is to utilize the archetypal and mythological insights of Jung to shed light on the meaning that the Gospel stories of Jesus have for our lives today. I have made statements that would have disturbed Jung because they go into the realms of metaphysics and theology, realms that Jung eschewed. I have not felt constrained to attempt exact faithfulness to Jung's many nuances in the meanings of terms such as *spirit* and *soul*. It may even be questioned whether Jung himself was completely consistent in his use of such words. Rather, I have been faithful to Jung in the way that he seemed to commend in his parable of the old man and the cave, in which Jung seemed to call each of us to do as he had done and find our own way. As James Yandell remarked in *The Imitation of Jung: An Exploration of the Meaning of Jungian* a Jungian is an individual, compelled by inner necessity to pursue the path of his own unfolding . . . [and] is one who *also* has found the work of Jung meaningful, and who experiences the values, attitudes, and concepts of analytical psychological as a congenial intellectual and emotional environment." Finally, Yandell quotes, and I echo, the words of the seventeenth-century Japanese poet Basho, "I do not seek to follow in the footsteps of the men of old; I seek the things they sought".[1]

▼

Contents

▼

HUMAN THOUGHT . . . only dimly discerns, it misdescribes, and it wrongly associates. But always there remain the same beacons that lure. Systems, scientific and philosophic, come and go. Each method of limited understanding is at length exhausted. In its prime each system is a triumphant success: in its decay it is an obstructive nuisance. The transitions to new fruitfulness of understanding are achieved by recurrence to the utmost depths of intuition for the refreshment of imagination.

—Alfred North Whitehead
Adventures of Ideas

IF, THEN, SOCRATES, we find ourselves in many points unable to make our discourse of the generation of gods and the universe in every way wholly consistent and exact, you must not be surprised. Nay, we must be well content if we can provide an account not less likely than another's; we must remember that I who speak, and you who are my audience, are but men and should be satisfied to ask for no more than the likely story.

—Plato
Timaeus

▼

Introduction

▼

BETWEEN THE MIDDLE AGES and the modern world lies a vast shift of interest. Plagued by fear and superstition, with a profound anxiety born of guilt, the people of those earlier centuries focused their attention on the problems of sin and damnation, God and devil, angels and demons. After the Renaissance and the Reformation, Francis Bacon, speaking as an unconscious bellwether of the future, announced that happiness in this present life was a valid concern and that the prediction and control of natural events through systematically applied human intelligence was the best means of attaining it. From this period the prevailing interest of the Western world became the exploration, observation, and control of the material world, in short, science and technology. Until the twentieth century, not much attention was given to the primary instrument of knowledge, the human psyche. Near the turn of the century when Freud announced the discovery of the unconscious, a new line of investigation began, and the field of modern psychology began to evolve. It is safe to say, however, that an immense tract of unexplored territory still lies ahead. The least known and most potent factors seem to lie in that zone that may be called the interface between religion and science. It is a zone that has been unpopular for a halfcentury or more, probably because of the negative climate created by positivism and Freud toward religion and despite the stellar work of William James and C. G. Jung.

Rather suddenly that climate of unpopularity has begun to

change. In the past two decades much intense work has been done
to understand the nature of the brain, although how the brain relates to consciousness is still a very open issue. Within the past two
decades a great interest has arisen in studying consciousness itself.
Certainly not least important has been the powerful suggestion
from the world of physics about the importance of consciousness in
the very creation of observable reality.

> With the awesome authority that we have given it, science is telling
> us that our faith has been misplaced. It appears that we have attempted
> the impossible, to disown our part in the universe. We have tried to do
> this by relinquishing our authority to the Scientists. To the Scientists
> we gave the responsibility of probing the mysteries of creation, change,
> and death. To us we gave the everyday routine of mindless living.
>
> The Scientists readily assumed their task. We readily assumed ours,
> which was to play a role of impotence before the ever-increasing com-
> plexity of "modern science" and the ever-spreading specialization of
> modern technology.
>
> Now, after three centuries, the Scientists have returned with their
> discoveries. They are as perplexed as we are (those of them who have
> given thought to what is happening).
>
> "We are not sure," they tell us, "but we have accumulated evidence
> which indicates that the key to understanding the universe is *you*."[1]

Another sharp shift in the climate of investigation is illustrated by
the insights of two American theologians reported in connection with
their reflections upon the so-called religious renewal of the 1950s in
the United States. In a probing essay written for publication in a
popular journal, Paul Tillich expressed concern for the loss of
"depth" in religion. He observed that not many people either inside
or outside the churches were asking the most serious and important
questions about the meaning and purpose of life. A few years later,
H. Richard Niebuhr, in an article for a widely circulated religious
magazine, reported his concern for the loss of meaning of the most
important of the Christian concepts, such as grace, sin, salvation,
heaven, and hell. Furthermore, argued Niebuhr, although what was
needed was the retranslation of these terms into forms that could
communicate with the modern mind, no such translation was possible without reference in one's immediate life experience to the expe-
riential realities to which earlier generations had applied these
traditional terms. What was lost, according to Niebuhr, was nothing

less than the religious experiences that alone could make sense of the otherwise empty terms. By adding Tillich's insight, we can see that the situation is even worse. People are not even asking the depth questions, to which, for an earlier generation, the religious terms had provided answers by directing people to the relevant religious experiences. Thus, Tillich and Niebuhr attested to the centrality of the symbolic life of the psyche in religion and in life and to the necessity of grounding that symbolism in the immediacy of experience rather than in floating abstract doctrine, where religious language can become words about words about words.

Perhaps the single most persistent investigator of the symbolic processes of the psyche has been the Swiss psychologist C. G. Jung. A man of great genius and industry, Jung applied himself unstintingly for six decades to his calling to investigate the human psyche. A deeply but not conventionally religious man, imbued with great scientific and philosophical acumen, Jung was impelled to include the religious domain as part and parcel of the functioning of psyche. He was also quite concerned about viewing the psyche as the organ of all knowing and realized that at the heart of his science was the problem of how the psyche could know itself. Like most wise people, Jung realized more and more how little we humans know of anything—least of all, ourselves, our own psyches.

Jung died two decades ago; since then, lavish amounts of observation and research have been poured into understanding ourselves. Yet, I must even more strongly echo Jung's awareness of our profound ignorance of ourselves: not only must we be aware of our ignorance but we must begin to gain deeper understanding. It is the human psyche that has its finger on the triggers of the nuclear weapons of the world, which can end all human life, if not *all* life on earth. It is the human psyche that must control the out-of-hand population increase of the world and end the pollution that threatens the biosphere.

My task in this book is to make a small contribution to that understanding and to do so by following the clues hinted at in the preceding discussion: the central importance of symbols in the psyche; their intimate connection with the depth questions of religion; and the relationship between symbols and our perception/creation of reality.

I

The Mysterious Psyche: Mythic and Rational

THE MOST AMAZING ORGANISM yet found in the universe is that creature called *homo sapiens.* The most sophisticated computer imaginable with the most advanced techniques available would not seriously rival the complexity of the brain of a human being. Yet, we are in large measure still a mystery to ourselves. The human psyche seems to rival the universe in its ability to exceed our mental grasp. The difficulty is multiplied when we try to study the psyche because the psyche is then studying itself.

Psyche is an ancient Greek word that is often translated as "soul" because it refers to the life principle, that which animates and makes alive. In Greek it also means "breath or spirit," for to the ancients, spirit, breath, and life were one principle. In more modern usage it has come to mean the sentient aspect of human life, comprising such aspects of ourselves as personality, soul, and mind and all the operations thereof, whether conscious or unconscious.

If for no other reason than its complexity, *psyche* would be difficult to define. It is now clear from neurological studies that the complexity of the brain is almost beyond imagining, much less understanding, and the psyche is far, far more than the brain. Our undertaking is not to understand in the sense of mastering psyche or bringing it into some rational scheme or rules. Rather our undertaking is to grasp what psyche is about, to orient ourselves to what we are in essence so that we can perceive human life in a new perspective, appreciating the mystery and power of the human pilgrimage.

The psyche is the source of all our knowing, doing, thinking, evaluating, feeling. It is the life center about which all human existence revolves. The home of the body is the psyche. Body is not just an aspect of psyche; rather, in the space-time dimension in which we have our existence, psyche expresses itself bodily—psyche is body.

The psyche is the key to knowing, and although philosophers have often investigated the ways of knowing, they seldom have considered that such work involved the psyche itself as the instrument of or for knowing. That is, philosophers often did not realize that they first had to develop a psychology, a theory of the psyche, before they could be critical of philosophical procedure in the study of knowing. This process is so circular that it seems well-nigh inescapable. Psychology scholars in the twentieth century have come to know how much, how very much, in the psyche occurs below, or beyond, the level of awareness and control. Any modern understanding of the human psyche must include the many and mysterious unconscious aspects that transcend conscious perception.

The most promising advances toward knowing ourselves have come from those who have taken the products or processes of the psyche as the beginning data and who have seen in the human psychic structure an analogy to the structure of the universe itself. A simplified statement of the rationale for these approaches is the view that the psyche, a natural process of the universe, can be fruitfully considered the universe's being conscious of itself. The psyche, in being conscious of the universe, of itself, has produced several schemes, several patterned ways of being conscious. One of these ways might be termed the cognitive or scientific way of knowing, e.g., our way of cognizing time and space. The other principal way of being conscious is appropriately termed the mythic way, or the symbolic way. These ways are "natural," albeit cultivated, ways of consciousness, and each has risen to a very high level of sophistication in human history.

The oldest, and I will argue, the most profound, way of being conscious is the mythic way, the symbolic way. The mythic way developed first and is the foundation of other forms, including the scientific, although myth itself benefits from feedback from the cognitive pattern. Of all the products of mankind, however, myth is surely the most incredible and mysterious for us moderns of the Western world (or parts of the world that have become Westernized, e.g., contemporary China and Japan). We are so alienated from the mythic way of knowing that we do not even consider it a way of knowing; the very term has become a misnomer for untruth. Placed beside the scientific, factual, or historical ways of consciousness and knowledge, myth is generally disregarded in the typical scholarly life of the West.

I will demonstrate that myth is by no means an invalid pattern of consciousness but an inherent and critically useful one. The Greeks gave us the terms *mythos* and *logos*. Each was a term for the concept "word." *Mythos* implied the image-evoking power of the word, its metaphorical, symbolic power. *Logos* referred to the cognitive content of the term, its logical (root, *logos*) meaning; the Latin term for the cognitive content is *ratio*, from which we derive *rational*. Any word (or most words) can function in either capacity, and we may interpret a word in either way, the rational or the mythic. These two ways seem to be the ends, or poles, of the conceptual continuum represented by language in its various forms.

It is useful in considering the human psyche to be aware that such a language or consciousness continuum exists. Each way of conceptualizing and presenting data falls somewhere on this continuum. Nearest the logos pole is the system of science; nearest the mythos pole is the realm of myth and religion. Other forms reach toward both poles and fall somewhere in between. History, biography, and media reporting are usually thought of as ideally near the logos pole. But, as we shall see, they, as well as science, include many mythic presuppositions. Poetry and fantasy, followed closely by novels and drama, fall near the mythic pole. But they, too, are somewhat shaped by the logos element or by feedback from it. Even relatively pure fantasy, such as that found in certain works of science fiction and the writings of Tolkien, contain elements from the logos pole. The psyche, from beyond consciousness, produces symbols and plots of mythic character, i.e., dreams, visions, fantasies, and rituals. With the aid of conscious reflection, these seem to be woven into the stories that live as the myths of the race, but myth is not a product of consciousness.

Joseph Campbell has observed that mythic language refers to the transcendent or the sacred and that its meaning concerns the ultimate issues of life and the questions of human and historical destiny. To speak about a people's symbol system, their myth, is then to speak about what lies at the very foundation of their being.

When we realize that a symbol system is the basis of religious thought, the symbol takes on overtly sacred value. We can then recognize that the task of myth is to speak of the ineffable, to make present to finite minds the Ultimate and Transcendent God. Myth is thus the very essence of revelation. Every myth is at the same time a product of human experience, imagination, fantasy, intuition, and, above all, inspiration. As Campbell has noted, it is a product of "divine seizure."

Campbell has also outlined four major functions of myth systems:

(1) to reconcile waking consciousness to the *mysterium tremendum et fascinans* of this universe *as it is.* . . .
(2) to render an interpretative total image of the same [the universe]. . . .
(3) the enforcement of a moral order: the shaping of the individual to the requirements of his geographically and historically conditioned social group. . . .
(4) [The most vital function:] to foster the centering and unfolding of the individual in integrity, in accord with . . . himself (the microcosm), . . . his culture (the mesocosm), . . . the universe (the macrocosm), and . . . that awesome ultimate mystery which is both beyond and within himself and all things.[1]

A mythological canon, or symbol system, is an organization of symbols, ineffable in import, by which the energies of aspiration are evoked and focused. Without a symbol system, the person, or a civilization, experiences emptiness and anxiety. Persons who have no symbol system experience a pervading sense of longing and searching, more or less frantic, for some way of filling the emptiness. We live in such a time, for the great mythologies of the past no longer evoke and gather the energies of aspiration that surge within us.

In the nineteenth century and the first half of the twentieth century, the general belief was that through the logical power of science, we were in contact with the real world. The errors of human perception were thought to be so well known that we could correct them. It was thus assumed that through the agency of microscopes, telescopes, other extensions of human sensory organs, and the corrective work of the rational power of the human mind, we had an accurate view of reality.

The twentieth century, particularly its second half, seems to mark one of those great turning points in the course of history that occur only every millennium or so. Shifts are denoted by the significant change in worldview, which underlies other cultural changes. The age that began with the breakup of the medieval mind-set and the revolutions in thought marked by the Renaissance, the Reformation, and the rise of the scientific-industrial culture, is drawing to a close. Because I will refer repeatedly to this age, a label will be useful. For simplicity but also because the term characterizes the main thrust of the thought of this period, this age will be referred to as the rationalistic age.

The rationalistic worldview was and is the general view of reality held in Western civilization by the scientifically unsophisticated mind, which means more than 99% of us, and was the reigning view among most scientists for the first half of the twentieth century. This way of conceiving reality was thereby socially approved not only as correct but the only correct view. For most, the very idea that this worldview was a human, and thus fallible, creation was heretical and abhorrent. The content of this worldview is essentially the Newtonian three-dimensional picture of solid objects occupying specific positions in vacuous space, immersed in the flow of time.

This way of perceiving separates the knower from the known, i.e., subject from object. The understanding of *truth* is that the object is accurately represented in the consciousness of the subject or in mathematical or other scientific formula. Although the scientific method climaxed in the early decades of this century, it has for some centuries been considered the one proper and correct means of knowledge.

A basic tenet of this position of science has been the claim of impartial objectivity, freedom from personal or even collective bias. Bacon believed that the scientific method would achieve this objectivity. He represents a decided break with the general tradition of the Middle Ages that was inherited from St. Augustine. In that tradition, objectivity commanded no particular regard because it was believed, as Augustine had taught, that the mind inherently knew the truth of reality: "Go not out of doors. Return into yourself; in the inner man dwells truth." Bacon reinvoked the necessity for sensory information, the collection of data through careful observation; by the time William James finished his *magnum opus*, *The Principles of Psychology*, he wrote to his brother, Henry, "I have to forge every sentence in the teeth of irreducible and stubborn facts."[2] The philosopher Alfred North Whitehead terms this the new color, or new tinge, of modern mentality.

What has happened since James is another revolution in thought and discovery, by virtue of which we recognize our personal role in the creation of those "stubborn and irreducible facts." We must now cease to speak of Reality as something quite apart from our processes of perception and data selection and begin to speak of the social and mythic construction of reality. (More will be said about perception later; for now, let us consider the terms *social* and *mythic*.)

Social refers primarily to culture; by *culture*, I do not mean the aristocratic sense of the elite but a particular stage of development of civilization and the characteristics that typify it, most particularly what we often speak of today as the *consciousness* or the worldview of a people who recognize their commonness through that worldview. Theodore Roszak says, "*Culture* is the embodiment of a people's shared reality, as expressed in word, image, myth, music, philosophy, science, moral style. *Reality* marks out the boundaries of what might be called the collective mindscape, the limits of sane experience."[3]

We are members of Western civilization of the twentieth cen-

tury because we have been acculturated into it. The journey from
mother's womb and breast through college is an indoctrination process. Carlos Castaneda's Don Juan said, "The world of everyday life
is not real, or out there as we believe it is. [Reality, or the world we
all know, is only a description,] a description that has been
pounded into [us] from the moment [of birth. Don Juan] pointed
out that everyone who comes into contact with a child is a teacher
who incessantly describes the world to him, until the moment
when the child is capable of perceiving the world as it is described. . . . From that moment on, however, the child is a *member*. He knows the description of the world."[4] For Don Juan, then,
the reality of our day-to-day life consists of an endless flow of
perceptual interpretations that we, the individuals who share a specific *membership*, have learned to make in common. This view then
becomes our taken-for-granted construction of reality; any other
view is regarded as wrong, even crazy. This view is now our *myth*,
or a part of our myth.

Before describing briefly the main characteristics of this myth, I
wish to reiterate in more detail what has been said about human
perception and interpretation, the way in which we proceed from
raw data to meaning. It has often been assumed, and is by most
people today, that we simply see what is out there to see. That is,
the objects we see and touch are presumed to be just what our
senses report to us. It seems quite certain, however, that such is
not the case. Perception is much more complicated, and the
achievement of meaning is much more subtle than the common
view implies.

The process from raw data to meaning is marked by at least two
notable coding, or interpretative, operations. The first of these is
performed by the nervous system itself. Visual or aural stimuli, for
example, are turned into electrical patterns in the nervous system.
We have almost no control over this process. Second, this electrical
information is transmitted to the brain, where it is again transformed. The simplest way of describing the second transformation
is to say that the electrical pattern is changed into a symbolic pattern. This second step seems to occur as follows: the pattern is compared with existing patterns that have been given symbolic names.

The incoming pattern is then named according to its family resemblance, and the name is taken to be the meaning of the pattern. For example, an object is seen by the eyes. The pattern of light and shadow calls forth a particular nervous response; upon comparison, the pattern seems to be like another pattern stored in the brain, so we call it a chair.

Kenneth Boulding has suggested that we can observe two distinct sets of stored patterns in the brain. One of these he calls images of fact, the other images of value. I prefer to call these sets of patterns *symbol systems* instead of images. So we can say that we have two symbol systems. The first of these symbol systems has to do with the nature of the sensible world. It is our picture, so to speak, of the way the world is, the physical and social systems that make up reality as we perceive it. This symbol system enables us to locate ourselves in physical and social reality and to have an idea of what is going on in those aspects of our world.

The second symbol system has to do with the value we put on a given situation or piece of data: important, desirable, commendable, urgent, dangerous, fearful. The second system is critical in making decisions because it represents all our priorities. For simplicity the first symbol system may be called the fact system, whose content is symbols of fact. The second may be called the value system, whose content is symbols of value. Every bit of incoming information from the nervous system is screened against these two sets of symbols, and they are, of course, interrelated. Data that seem to fit easily into some aspect of the fact system are so labeled and passed on to the value system for evaluation and decisions. If data do not fit, they may be rejected as mere noise or error, or they may be called mystery and stored for later consideration.

If a sufficient mass of data conflicts with the system, some revision in the system itself is called for. But there is great reluctance to make changes in the basic assumptions. These symbol systems are like old and familiar friends—they are the very stuff of our lives. Letting them go is painful and upsetting. It disturbs our sense of stability and introduces ambiguity and uncertainty. Hence, we do not change unless forced to do so by internal or external discord. Usually, significant learning merely adds to the system. We are rarely called upon to make major changes in our interpretative symbol systems and when we are, the experience is traumatic. The very stability of the world seems at stake.

For example, look at the reluctance of the authorities of the Middle Ages to let go of the cosmology of Ptolemy or the reluctance of culture to let go of the idea that the world was only recently created by God and in just the form we find it today. The idea that the earth might be of vast age and that life forms might once have been different from their current forms seemed to threaten the very source of life.

Hence, when I say that the rationalistic age is drawing to a close, I am talking about a watershed in history. All such watersheds are marked by great social unrest. The American sociologist P. A. Sorokin has catalogued these times of unrest rather carefully. The twentieth century shows up as particularly disturbed. Sorokin's data, which first appeared in the early 1940s, were alarming but also very puzzling because the age of rationality, i.e., the rationalistic worldview, could not account for the disturbance. Civilization was supposed to be getting better as people got more rational, more educated, more enlightened.[5]

All of us have been nurtured in the rationalist symbol system and the value system that accompanies it. Our very perception of reality is thoroughly, almost totally, conditioned by that symbol system. The way we perceive the makeup of the universe, the values we espouse, the meaning we attach to our lives is largely a product of the symbol system we have learned and chosen for ourselves.

One final note about the importance of a cultural symbol system. Because that symbol system provides a culturally approved way of viewing life and the world, it necessarily marks a person's boundaries of reality. One who perceives something different from what is usually perceived by persons of that culture is likely to be considered insane or, at best, odd. For example, in our culture, it is not normal to hear voices when there are neither persons nor electronic devices about. Even less normal is the seeing of visions. Hence, one who has such experiences and consults a rationalistic doctor about them will likely soon be under psychiatric care. The chief purpose of the latter will be to normalize the patient's worldview so that he or she no longer sees and hears what others do not.

We need desperately to know the character of the rationalistic symbol system for two reasons: first, it marks the bounds of reality and has been our primary source of understanding and meaning; second, because it is falling apart, we had best understand what it is that we must relinquish. The age has four main characteristics:

(1) a distrust of the natural and nonrational

(2) a rejection of the spiritual dimension

(3) an emphasis on this world—history, economics, politics

(4) a basic trust in human rationality

These characteristics might also be described as four dichotomies demanded by the symbol system and presumed to be part of reality itself. They also represent values that are implicit in the symbol system:

(1) rational versus nonrational

(2) matter versus spirit

(3) objective (this world) versus subjective (imaginary, or otherworldly)

(4) fact versus myth

The first term of each dichotomy is the real, or preferred, according to the rationalistic view.

Largely following the lead of Descartes, Newton, and Locke, the nineteenth century saw the full flowering of rationalism in the philosophy known as positivism. The term *positivism* comes from the doctrine of the German philosopher Auguste Comte, who asserted that the highest form of knowledge is the simple description of sensory phenomena. Comte advocated an evolutional law of three stages of mankind: the earliest, the *theological*, in which anthropomorphic wills were used to explain natural events; next, the *metaphysical*, in which these wills were depersonalized and became forces and essences; and last, the *positive*. Positivism is important because, in a relatively naïve form, it became the pattern of the scientific myth, which was most popular through the mid-twentieth century and which still largely captivates the mind of the man in the street. Positivistic description was supposed to result in

mathematical formulas, not introspective psychological data.
Comte knew almost nothing about how the human mind operates.
His theory is naïve when set beside our current understanding of
the processes and limits of rationality and perception. Yet Comte's
view is built into the reigning mythology of our civilization. Small
wonder it is collapsing.

The development of the age of rationalism runs like an arrow
from the Renaissance through the rise of the scientific worldview
up through the nineteenth century. The so-called Enlightenment
was the cultural outgrowth of the change in mythology that was taking place in the populace as a whole. The Enlightenment was the
public announcement that a new myth had been enthroned. From
that time, the rationalistic mentality rapidly became the background tone for all endeavors of Western civilization.

Even before Comte and the development of positivism, the romantic movement, associated with such names as the German
Goethe and the English William Blake, was a great protest against
the tide of rationalism, although a protest that was not heard. The
emerging worldview of the late twentieth century is learning much
from the romantics. The romantic protest was a valid criticism of
the unnecessary and foolish conception of the rationalists, which resulted in narrowing the horizon of knowledge to the rational. The
romantics saw the universe as living and sentient, the product of
Spirit. Real knowledge of the universe, they believed, came by way
of the emotional and intuitional; fullness of feeling and experience
were necessary aspects of knowing. Knowing is living, and the philosopher must approach nature through inspiration, longing, and
sympathy. We neither can nor should return to the doctrines of the
romantics, but we must learn the basis of their protest against the
rationalistic system. They understood very well what was being cast
aside in the rationalistic tide.

Small wonder that in our day it has become obvious that rationalism is grotesque. Science itself has in many respects led the way
beyond rationalism. The first significant breakthroughs came from
the fields of physics and mathematics. The neat mechanistic universe necessary to positivism and rationalism was wiped out by the
discoveries of the first quarter of the twentieth century. Relativity,

the quantum theory, the electromagnetic nature of matter, the principle of indeterminacy made any notion such as positive knowledge incredible. In mathematics it became apparent that there were multiple competing systems of logic, with no final choice of right or wrong.

We are awakening to the realization that our scientific endeavors have not enlightened us about values and not told us nearly so much as we had thought about the nature of the world. Harold Schilling, a physicist, once commented in a lecture that we are, in fact, increasing the mystery of the universe faster than we are increasing our knowledge of it. Each new answer that we establish enables us to ask several new questions; consequently, expressed proportionally, we know less with each new discovery.

The emerging worldview denies each of the four dichotomies upheld by the rationalistic age, and they are seen as a fundamental cause of the evils inherent in the passing age. Indeed, the new worldview sees that instead of dichotomies, the universe is composed of polarities. It is no longer believable that the best, much less the only, way of knowledge is the rational.

With the rationalistic myth/symbol system, we constructed a mechanistic reality; it could be described mathematically and predictably because no freedom or will was involved. The body of knowledge created through this form of consciousness is defective as a description of the universe. Its mathematical laws do not describe what happens at the macroscopic or the subatomic levels of space-time. The emerging myth/symbol system, or worldview, brings a new possibility of consciousness and knowledge. The new possibility for consciousness is to "know" in a mythically founded style, a transrational knowing. Any form of knowing, reality construction, is mythically founded. The selection and the perception of what are called raw data are already guided by mythic assumptions and personal interests. The method of investigation construes the data in a certain way because there are no data without presuppositions. Pure objectivity is, and always has been, an unattainable ideal. The new form of knowledge, which we can now create, will be self-conscious and critical of its mythic foundations. In that knowledge will be recognition of the transrational nature of myth, yet awareness that rationality must be used to criticize, test, and explain myth—not, however, to replace or create myth.

What happens, then, to hard facts, solid matter, and how can the concept God be included? Facts, the supposed creations of rationality, are in every case built upon the foundation of symbol systems—myths. That is, a fact can be regarded as true only within the bounds of a specific symbol system, a certain way of viewing reality. Matter, we know now in a new symbol system, is a pattern of dancing energy. *Energy* is a desacralized term for God, or for a major characteristic of God, namely, the ability to make things happen, and the essential nature of what is happening. Perhaps we can say that *energy* is the rationalized term for God, all that can be left when the rational process has finished its arbitrary stripping away.

The new worldview is not afraid of Spirit, nor does it regard it as less than matter. Both are energic phenomena. In nature, that is, nonsentient nature, energy appears in crystalline forms, or rhythmic patterns. We call these forms by various names, such as electrons, atoms, molecules, cells. In these forms, energy moves unceasingly in cycles or waves. One wave breaks upon the shore to be followed by another, world without end. Out of its endless wave motions, energy produces hierarchical patterns. When these are sufficiently long-lived to be detected by human means, we perceive them as crystals, or persistent shapes.

Thought process, or the symbols of the mind, are likewise modes of patterned energy. Most interesting of all is the realization that these symbol constructs of the mind exhibit patterns that often parallel the crystalline forms found in nature. In the old rationalistic worldview, these patterns in the mind were purely subjective and hence nonsense, nonrational, nonfactual, if they referred to the external world of matter. If they referred to the so-called spiritual world, they were doubly condemned as meaningless statements about a nonentity.

According to the emerging worldview, the spiritual is the *inside*, or the other side of the material. The spiritual is the domain of meaning, purpose, value, choice, perception, enjoyment. The spiritual is preeminently the real of the symbolic, the mythic. Religion and myth are indissolubly connected. *Religion* derives from the Latin *ligare*, which means "to connect, or tie." It is related to the English word *rely*, which means "trust or depend upon." Religion is that which we take with ultimate seriousness because it ties us to our foundation. As we have seen, myth is the founding of culture. It is also the founding of meaning for any individual. Thus, religions must be intimately connected to myth. Religion is the practice by which we express the seriousness with which we are taking our myth, i.e., our symbol system. But when one's myth becomes otiose, or even fractures a bit, meaning slips out the door and morals are only moments behind. A myth can be held religiously only by those who believe it as an explanation of the cosmos they experience.

Before the nineteenth century, especially in the archaic world before the Greeks, myth was not regarded as it is now in the vernacular, i.e., a story that is not true; quite the contrary, myths were believed to express truth. Mircea Eliade in his *Myths, Dreams and Mysteries*, indicates that the ancient peoples regarded myth as very precious because it was sacred, contained exemplary models for human behavior, and revealed the truth about humanity and reality. I shall be using *myth* to mean a pattern of symbols, sometimes literary, that gives sense, meaning, and value to life. Persons may or may not be self-conscious of this myth.

In particular, myth addresses those most important questions of life to which science offers almost no contribution: What is the source and purpose of human existence? Why the universe? How am I and how are we to live in relation to the Ultimate, to the world and to each other? How does one choose the right vocation and how does it relate to the purpose of life?

Science itself is dependent on myth in ways that are not often recognized. Alfred North Whitehead describes one element of this dependency as the contribution of the medieval faith, "the inexpugnable belief that every detailed occurrence can be correlated with its antecedents in perfectly definite manner, exemplifying general principles.[6] Whitehead credits this belief to the medieval faith in the rationality of God. Faith in the very *possibility* of science is an unconscious derivative from medieval theology.

My intention in this book is to give no more than a few crucial insights into the rise of science; rather, I hope to present a more

accurate understanding of the process of creating human knowledge. Every culture consists in the main of a stock of myths that
guides its functions by establishing a characteristic way of perceiving reality and responding to it. This stock of myth is very resistant
to change and virtually impervious to intentional change. Yet, at
the same time, it is observable that we are in the midst of a shift in
myth that is already precipitating shifts in the patterns of culture.

The psyche may be viewed as a language phenomenon, provided we define language very broadly to include every form of
communication with ourselves and with others. Language, as has
been noted, may be viewed as a continuum between myth and fact,
between symbols and signs. The end of the continuum called fact,
or sign, is mostly used for rational thought and communication, including science. This form of language includes several elements,
but our concern is the sign. We need to distinguish the sign both
from the signal and from the symbol. A *signal* functions with or
without consciousness to announce the event for which it is a signal. Thunder is a signal of lightning, as smoke is of fire. The *sign* is
an intentional communicative device (word, gesture, grimace)
whose meaning is established by convention. Convention, of
course, simply means the common practice of the users of the language. Conventional meanings are culturally or socially established
and are maintained through socialization.

Now we come to the *symbol*, a much more mysterious phenomenon. The symbol shares with the sign its material nature, i.e., a
word, gesture, or grimace, but there the resemblance ends. A symbol represents something that is significantly unknown and perhaps
unknowable in any full sense. Jung says, "A symbol always presup-
poses that the chosen expression is the best possible description or
formulation of a relatively unknown fact, which is none the less
known to exist or is postulated as existing."[7] Jung was very concerned about keeping the conception of symbol quite distinct from
that of sign and allegory. He believed that such confusion was
widespread and that it was reductive and misleading for scientific
thought. Freud, in keeping with his positivism in general, sought
systematically to reduce symbols to signs.

Paul Tillich described six characteristics of a symbol:

(1) It refers beyond itself to something else, as does a sign.

(2) The symbol participates in the reality to which it points. As an example, he mentions the flag, which participates in the power and dignity of the nation it represents. This "participation" is a difficult concept, somewhat akin to the Christian doctrine of the real presence of Christ, or transubstantiation, in the sacrament of communion. Another way of explaining the characteristic would be to speak of the symbol as making present the reality for which it stands. This character is a primary source of symbolic power. In the presence of the symbol, one is, in fact, in the presence of the reality; the symbol serving as a conduit, as it were.

(3) The symbol "opens up levels of reality which are otherwise closed for us." The symbol here functions as a tool or a key; without its representational power, our minds have no grasp on the subject. Art takes us far beyond the realm penetrable by logic.

(4) This penetration is true not only for the world but for the human soul as well. As Tillich writes, "A great play gives us not only a new vision of the human scene, but it opens up hidden depths of our own being."

(5) Symbols are not created, nor can they be created, "*intentionally.*" "They grow out of the individual or collective unconscious and cannot function without being accepted by the unconscious dimension of our being."[8] Jung expressed this aspect similarly but with some added insight. "An expression that stands for a known thing remains a mere sign and is never a symbol. It is, therefore, quite impossible to create a living symbol, i.e., one that is pregnant with meaning, from known associations. For what is thus produced never contains more than was put into it. Every psychic product, if it is the best possible expression at the moment for a fact as yet unknown or only relatively unknown, may be regarded as a symbol. . . . Since every scientific theory contains an hypothesis, and is therefore an anticipatory description of something still essentially unknown, it is a symbol."[9] He also says the symbol is a product of the unconscious and that data from every psychic function go into its making.

(6) The final characteristic mentioned by Tillich is that symbols cannot be invented. Rather "like living beings, they grow and they

die."[10] Jung speaks similarly but adds data and detail about the birth and death of symbols. As we study the symbol in more detail, we will consider further its creation and dynamics.[11]

One added note on symbols, this mainly from Ernst Cassirer: Without language, but especially without symbols, there cannot be any organized or definite reality, any world at all. "Myth, art, language, and science appear as symbols in the sense of forces each of which produces and posits a world of its own. In these realms the spirit exhibits itself in that inwardly determined dialectic by virtue of which alone there is any reality, any organized and definite Being at all. . . . [T]he special symbolic forms are . . . *organs* of reality, since it is solely by their agency that anything real becomes an object for intellectual apprehension, and as such is made visible to us."[12]

Clearly, symbols lie at the heart of human existence and perception, and symbols are connected in a meaningful way to form myths. Myths are not simply idle stories, but are the very root of human consciousness, the fount from which meaning flows, the basis of "creating reality" both socially and individually. Wherever we come across living myth, myth that is functioning in the lives of people, we are in religious territory. Myth is preeminently the language of faith. As Paul Tillich observed, "faith, understood as the state of being ultimately concerned, has no language other than symbols."[13] Only the nonfunctioning myth, the dead myth, or the myth from which we are alienated is not a matter of faith. That faith may, of course, be very secular, even atheistic, but wherever there is meaningful life, there is faith and thus myth. Myth, after all, is believed by faith, i.e., it cannot be proved by rational means, although as I will explain later, there are some criteria for evaluating myth. In the modern world, along with our rejection of myth has gone our realization that, nonetheless, we still live by myth, and in that respect are still very religious. Our myths have simply been stated so that they look like science or reason or commonsense.

In the ancient world, religion was at the forefront of human existence and the social order, as it was in colonial America. The myths of any given religion were usually collected formally or informally in some recognizable body of literature. These ancient collections present a surprisingly uniform view of the purpose of human existence. The primary insight of all the major world religions and most of the primitive religions is that the purpose of human existence is a religious pilgrimage, a journey. The journey is variously described, but its destination is union with a divine source that is in, with, and under everything. The human religious pilgrimage is a journey to God in life and time. The journey is experienced and described in rich symbolism, lived and understood in the images of symbolic language.

The human being comes with only a few programmed responses, e.g., an aversion to height, fear of falling, the suckling response to the nipple, and, of course, the autonomic responses such as heartbeats, breathing. Many psychologists have argued from these facts that the human is born a *tabula rasa,* the brain a clean slate ready for experience to write upon. More modern investigations, however, have cast serious doubt on such theory. Jung demonstrated that the human psyche is, at birth, already possessed of a specific structure common to the human species; it is a collective phenomenon. Everyone in the world has fingerprints, but the fingerprints of each person are unique.

This innate psychic structure is most easily conceptualized as a common predisposition to form images that relate to the structure of the psyche and its dynamics. To the predisposing structural elements, Jung gave the name *archetype.* He compared the psychic archetype with that element, in such substances as water, which causes the substance to take on, under appropriate conditions, a particular crystalline structure. The archetypal structure best known to us is the ego, the center of our consciousness, or perhaps the screen on which all our perceptible experience is observed. The main story of the psyche, and hence of myth, concerns the way ego relates to the other archetypal (structural) elements of the psyche.

The first half of life, roughly up to age thirty-five, is concerned with the development and independence of ego from its birthplace in the unconscious aspect of the psyche. This part of the story is the tale of the development of consciousness, with ego as its center. The second half of life concerns the reconnections of ego, now inde-

pendent, to the ground of its being, the great unconscious or transpersonal psyche, but particularly to the center of the whole psyche,
which Jung called the Self. The Self is the most important archetypal element; it pervades the psyche and is the senior partner in
the fellowship of the psyche. The junior partner is the ego. And
here lies a big problem, because, after its adventure of coming to
independence through much hardship, ego usually also comes to
presume that it is the senior partner, if not the only intelligent part
of the psyche. This individualistic stance is particularly endemic in
Western civilization. In fact, one may construe most of the history
of the West as the story of this development of a strong and independent ego. Our stress on freedom, our overemphasis on rationality as *the* way of knowing, even our drift away from religion—all
can be traced to this pattern.

This pattern of the development of consciousness has a great
deal to do with the language and with the symbols of the culture as
well. The dominant symbols of a culture point to its basic conceptions about persons, nature, the ultimate purposes of life (which
traditionally meant God or the gods), and the appropriate or desirable relations between these. In developed cultures, these foundational understandings are elaborated into social systems of
considerable complexity, but even simple or primitive cultures are
founded upon such visions of the nature and meaning of human existence vis-à-vis the Ultimate.

Many foundational understandings, dominant cultural myths,
are not set forth in specific documents but form the undergirding
motifs of the culture. For example, the Middle Ages in western
and eastern Europe can be well characterized as an age of faith.
The foundational understanding came directly from the Christian
religion, albeit in practice modified considerably by the older religions of central Europe. The ultimate purpose of life was salvation, i.e., reunion with God, and the way of salvation was through
the ministrations of the church. Consequently, the building of
churches and the affairs of the church were the focus of the culture. For complex reasons, that unified culture began to fragment, but central to that fragmentation was a change in the
foundational understanding, the myth. The focus shifted from the

next world to this, from heaven to earth, from God to man, from church to world, from faith to knowledge and skill. Hence, there were vast changes not only in conceptions about the world but in the values by which people lived. In terms of the language continuum described earlier, the shift was away from the mythic pole and toward the logos pole. As we shall see, along with the shift came the notion that true knowledge belongs only to the logos pole, the realm of ego-conscious rationality.

Religious literature warns us against this arrogant claim of the ego to the mastery of the psyche, but it speaks in mythic, symbolic language whose referents we often misread. For example, consider Jesus' parable of the wicked husbandmen who, in effect, claimed ownership of the vineyard because their master, the owner, had gone away on a trip to another country. The punch line warns that the tenants who had claimed mastery will be put to death. The ego, claiming mastery over the psyche, is setting itself up for a great fall, and not all the king's horses and all the king's men may be able to put it back together again.

The goal in personality development is not the strong ego, master of its soul and captain of its fate. The goal for the ego is to have good rapport with the depths of the psyche. Only an ego in good rapport can help compensate for the ups and downs of psychic life. Only such an ego can perform well its task of relating inner and outer realms and their quickly shifting demands.

The paramount tool that one has to work with in life is one's self. In the helping and service professions, self-knowledge is indispensable; no amount of time and effort is too much to invest in attaining and maintaining wholeness. It is increasingly evident that most personal and collective failures in science, politics, economics, education, and religions, indeed in every aspect of social order, are due to problems of the psyche. The culture and its individuals cry out for deliverance, for wholeness. The movement toward wholeness, I argue, is properly understood as the religious pilgrimage, the journey to God.

The thesis of this chapter is that the essential nature of the human is to live by myth or to be lived by myth. The essence of the psyche is its processing of mythic symbols.

The circle symbolizes wholeness, unity, completeness.

This circle, representing the psyche, is broken to show that it is not yet complete. What words will help describe the psyche? The psyche is a relational phenomenon that takes up a relationship with itself. It is a relationship, as is every occasion of the universe. The same is true in the view that modern physics takes of the physical universe. A universal quality of the psyche is that it takes up a relationship with itself. It does this by bringing into being a secondary, derivative center.

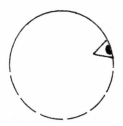

This second center may be thought of as an eye, a center of perception. It perceives both externally and internally, outwardly and inwardly.

Its perception, however, is not direct in either domain. It is analogous to the pilot of a sealed spaceship whose only contact is through a computer. The computer has two screens. One seems to be in some way correlated with the world outside the spaceship. The other screen seems to be more correlated with what is going on in the ship and in the computer. Simply, our data both from "outside" and from "inside" appear to consciousness already coded. The terms *inside* and *outside* are arbitrary. Conventionally, those words are used in a spatial sense. The wine is inside the jug until it is poured, then it is outside the jug. The psyche, however, is in no way like a jug, which contains its contents. The realm of the psyche is the realm of spirit, a realm whose spatial location is indeterminable. The psyche simply appears to consciousness and is discriminable by consciousness from the nonspirit world of daily events in space-time. The world of psyche beyond consciousness is in no way nonobjective or purely subjective or not real. For convenience, *outside* and *external* will be used to mean the perceptual world inferred as not being part of the individual's psyche. The data about external relations are coded by our perceptual physiology, translated from heat, cold, red, hard, rough, into electrical patterns and then into chemical patterns. Each step represents a condensation and a coding of the data. The final coding is then compared with stored patterns and given meaning. The stored patterns are our myth.

The data about internal relations are also coded, appearing on the screen of the ego in the form of dreams (day and night), vision, intentions, wants, and desires, whether negative or positive. All these are the stuff of myth. The code is a symbolic one.

So, both in its external relations and in its internal relations, the psyche lives mythically, i.e., understands by means of myth. Consciousness *is* mythic. Hence, we all live or are lived by myths. Freud brought this to light for the modern world when he discovered that many of his clients seemed to live out the Oedipus myth. Gradually, it is becoming clear that the myths live in all of us because they represent the deep structures of the human psyche. The myths are visual or verbal symbols of psychic components. As noted, Jung called these components *archetypes*. The psyche is composed of archetypes, each with its own character and potentials. The ego is an archetype of the psyche, and its life is governed by its relation to the other archetypes of the psyche.

The archetypes have been considered godlike powers because they are experienced that way. Archetypes do not manifest themselves directly but reveal themselves in images. The images are the symbols of that archetype. Their manifestation is always somewhat awesome, numinous, an experience of the sacred, of spiritual power and fascination. Classical myth is a kind of catalog of these experiences. For example, the Greeks told the story of Eros (Cupid, Amor), the god of love. The person struck by Cupid's arrow fell helplessly in love. Is that not a good description of falling in love? There is no choosing of the object of love, no will, intention,

or control of the person or the time. Falling in love seems to be
brought about by an agency beyond our control. And the loved one
almost literally glows with the radiance of Amor, as Moses glowed
with the radiance of Jahweh when he returned from the top of
Mount Sinai with the tablets of the Commandments.

So the ego perceives through myth and is lived by myth. Perceiving through myth is strongly affected by one's culture. Every
culture is gathered and held together by shared myth.

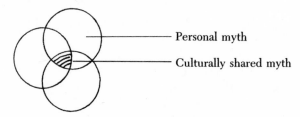

Personal myth

Culturally shared myth

The culturally shared myth is the basis on which a society creates
its view of reality.[14] The individual, however, lives only in part in
the shared myth. Not only do we have our personal myth, but the
gods within—the archetypal forces—are continually at work, shaping and reshaping the myths we are living. Each of us must get in
touch with our personal myths and become aware of the culturally
shared myth; beyond that, we must become sensitive to the demands of the archetypal forces, the realm of spirit.

One's relation to the personal myth and the shared myth is best
described by the word *faith*. Faith is an attitude of trust and loyalty
toward or invested in. The object to which the faith is directed is a
god. For, as Luther noted, faith and trust of the heart make both
God and the idols. The myths that we live are the manifestation of
the God or gods who have grasped our hearts and minds. We shape
our world; i.e., we create reality to suit the myths.

Under the aegis of rationalistic materialism, ego has come to be
perceived as the master of psyche and has even become confused
with soul. Even worse, ego has been limited as effective in knowing
only through its rational capacity. Intuition, mythic or mystic vision, poetic and esthetic insight, along with all other spiritual functions, have been radically devalued. How can we find a new way of

consciousness, one that is more adequate, that properly includes dimensions discarded by rationalistic materialism? A first step is to grasp more accurately how our consciousness is formed and what symbol system we can use to be appropriately conscious of our consciousness.

II

The Transformation Key

EACH PERSON creates the world in the images of his or her own symbol system; the symbol system is one's myth. Every language system (game) has its own overt or implied symbol system. In the context of this book, a language system does not mean English or French because these are not sufficiently different from each other. But to go from English to Hopi or to Japanese changes one's way of being able to perceive the world. Languages reflect within their structure a particular mythic way of creating the perceived world. Even sharper differences are noted if the shift is from one symbol/myth system to another. A shift to another system represents a shift from one state of consciousness to another, i.e., a fundamentally different way of creating the perceived world.

The two foundations of every human expression are experience and language, i.e., a symbol/myth system in which we have and express the experience. *Experience* means everything that manifests itself to consciousness in any way, including dream, vision, fantasy, hallucination, extrasensory perception, as well as experiences of what is usually called the world, others, or events.

Experience may be presumed to occur also to the unconscious aspect of psyche. If we accept Jung's distinction of a personal and the transpersonal (or collective) unconscious, one's life experience is a principal content of the personal unconscious. The transpersonal aspect of psyche is not known directly but manifests itself through symbols and affects; thus, we know very little, almost nothing, about the direct effects of experience upon the transpersonal psyche. Certainly the transpersonal psyche does receive and respond to experience. Jung proposed that it responds in a compensatory fashion, with the purpose of guiding the person toward her or his destiny. I will discuss experience only as it relates to consciousness and, to a lesser degree, to the personal unconscious. The purpose in this chapter is to clarify the basic dynamics of conscious knowing, i.e., world creating.

An experience is always so much shaped by the interpretive symbol system that we more properly speak of "experiencing as" rather than just experiencing. The symbol/myth system has a structure that gives shape to experiencing so that we perceive meaningfully; i.e., we *experience* something or some situation *as a particular kind of experience.* The personal emphasis, or the personal orientation, of the experiencer adds its unique flavor to modify or emphasize some aspect of the general cultural symbol system. One who sees life's meaning in terms of sex or power will construe every experience in terms of this dominant concern.

To know at all is to know in some symbol/myth system. To shift from one system to another is to "create" the world in a different way; i.e., one *experiences* the world *as* different. This shift is often called an experience of an altered state of consciousness. That terminology is no problem unless one means by it that the world "out there" remains the same and only one's perception changes. The term *world* means our experiencing or creating of the world. To speak of the world out there is an error; it is the dichotomy of Descartes, an artificial division, an abstraction from our experience.

Once we realize that we do in fact create the world through the means of a symbol/myth system and that there are alternative symbol/myth systems, how do we choose among them? In our culture, which is probably the most highly developed in terms of consciousness of any known culture, living or dead, most people still have not reached a level at which they can raise this question, at least not in any critical form. The average person simply lives out life within the dominant symbol/myth system of the culture, not realizing that significant alternatives exist. Hence, as Lawrence Kohlberg has noted in regard to moral reasoning, most members of American society are in the conventional stage, essentially "other-directed," or rule-oriented. They have not realized the arbitrary nature of the rules of society.

The equivalent position in religious orientation is orthodoxy of some variety. In orthodoxy, as well as the conventional stage, an external authority either is an essential part of the symbol/myth system or supports and authorizes the symbol/myth system. This authority may be mother, father, the law, pope, priest, or Bible. With this orientation the deeper faith question—whom or what can I finally trust?—is never significantly raised because it has been prematurely foreclosed by the granting of absolute authority to someone, something, some organization. This position is also held by what Robert Bellah has termed the secular orthodox, a term meaning about the same as *positivist*. The secular orthodox rejects all religious ideas as false or merely subjective but accepts as true any idea that comes through the "scientific" symbol/myth system that he or she holds.

It is beyond the scope of this book, and indeed would require a whole book, to discuss fully this very important question of the criteria for choosing a symbol/myth system, but Ian Barbour, in his *Myths, Models and Paradigms*, discusses this issue somewhat extensively and refers to much of the relevant literature.[1] Barbour, however, has not grasped the notion of a continuum of language systems from myth to fact language, nor does he seem to have grasped that the source of our symbols is the creative unconscious, the transpersonal psyche.

Both in science and in philosophy, particularly metaphysics, modern thinkers have become aware of this choosing among theoretical systems. In science the choice is usually thought of as the search for a theory. In metaphysics, the problem more nearly parallels the choice of a myth/symbol system, for in metaphysics the search is for a comprehensive system of thought that will explain the gamut of human experience. As has been noted, cultures also make such choices, though with little or no awareness that the choices are being made. Until this century, we had little critical knowledge about the means or the method of such cultural choices.

In biblical scholarship, the great New Testament professor Dr. Rudolf Bultmann, of Germany, began to point out nearly fifty years ago that there was more to New Testament interpretation than explaining the text—one first had to understand the way of knowing that the authors had presumed. Bultmann chose the existential analytic of Martin Heidegger as his tool for unlocking the way of knowing found in the New Testament; unfortunately, he did not realize that this chosen symbol system was also mythic (as any symbol system must be) and thus confused the issue by speaking of "demythologizing" as his method.

Bultmann chose Heidegger's analytic because he thought it was a "neutral," or scientific, analytic and that it was the best description available of human existence. That is, Bultmann chose Heidegger on the basis of the psychology that the system presented because any explanation of human existence and behavior is necessarily a psychology either by intent or by implication. Heidegger's work *Sein und Zeit [Being and Time]* is indeed a psychology, albeit a somewhat metaphysical one, and one whose empirical foundations are rather unclear.

The choice among competing symbol/myth systems, when lifted to the conscious level, includes the consideration of such factors as adequacy, appropriateness, internal or self-consistency, and elegance. William of Occam took a major step in devising criteria for elegance when he spoke of the necessity and virtue of simplicity (entities are not to be multiplied except as may be necessary). But elegance is composed of something more than simplicity—something that might be called novelty or diversity—that is, if simplicity can in some measure be equated with harmony or order. A kind of divine tension exists between these two great principles of the universe, harmony and diversity. Too much harmony, too much order, leads to controlled sterility like that observable in Russia today, and it may occur in all realms of life, political, biological, social, or botanical; for example, witness the threat of environmental disaster through our attempts to control the natural world. Too much novelty is equally unstable. The majority of life mutations are not viable; many are monstrous. That is why the proposal to create new life forms in genetic research is so fraught with hazard. Creating

new life forms has the potential, however remote, of creating a
plague for which we have no cure—relatively instant homicide.

The adequacy of a symbol system is its ability to accommodate
data, i.e., explain or make sense of every phenomenon known to
us. Quite a task! Yet, if we know something, we know it in some
symbol system, so the most adequate of all symbol systems would
be the system *of* symbol systems, i.e., a metasymbol system whose
task is to understand symbol systems. Inasmuch as a symbol system
is involved every time we know, the most useful and adequate symbol system would be a metapsychology, i.e., a metasystem to describe the nature of the human psyche, because the psyche is the
instrument of knowing. Such a system would have to take the natural symbols of the psyche for its foundational symbols because they
are the empirical data provided by the thing to be known. Thus,
the natural symbols of the psyche are the most empirical data available for the study of the psyche, more basic and less abstract than
the so-called higher levels of knowing, namely, rational knowing,
or cognition.

The appropriateness of a symbol system is its ability to translate
experience into knowing with minimal slippage. More accurately, it
is the way the symbols express the richness of the experience without undue distortion of it. In the psyche a naturally appropriate
symbol system represents the archetypes of the psyche—appropriate because it is the way the archetypes manifest themselves. As
noted, archetypes are embodied in consciousness in the form of a
symbol, which Jung called an archetypal image. The archetype itself is never directly observable. Because archetypes shape human
experience, the most useful and critical data for an appropriate
metasymbol system come from a study of the archetypal images as
manifested not only in dream but in the mythic lore of the race.
The archetypal symbols are the primary structuring elements of
human experience and are remarkably similar in many cultures.

While one is undergoing a rich experience, one can rarely reflect critically on the experience at the same time. Critical reflection comes as a secondary process. The experience is somehow
recorded so that it can be an object of reflection later. One then
tries to sort out its meaning, i.e., seek the appropriate symboliza-

tion. At the outset the experiencing process was shaped by the functioning myth symbol system of the individual. Now, in this second, reflective stage, the attempt is to bring to full consciousness the meaning implicit in the original experience. Varying types of language—poetic, historical, scientific—may be tested for their capacity to express or expound meaning.

The *natural* language of meaning, a spontaneous language of the psyche itself, is found to be the content of dreams, visions, and myths throughout the human race. Its symbols are found in every world language with astounding regularity. Jung traced the source of this regularity to the common, universal structure of the psyche. The people of the prehistoric world lived out their existence in a world structured by this natural language of the psyche. We call their structure mythology. The myth they lived was not chosen in any intentional way; it happened to them. In the same fashion, we do not choose our dreams or fantasies. The unique structure of this natural language of the psyche is not so much in its linguistic grammar as in its symbolic grammar. Claude Lévi-Strauss, a French anthropologist, showed the nature and the universality of the linguistic grammatical structure. Jung studied the symbolic grammatical structure and demonstrated its universality. A universal structure of symbols parallels, or is appropriate to, the dynamics of the psyche in its developmental process. The referent of this natural symbol system, which is the structure of myth, is the psyche itself in its various dynamic states. The natural symbols, as Jung demonstrated, refer to the structuring elements of the psyche, which he termed *archetypes*.

The dynamic relationships of archetypes within the psyche produce the particular state of the psyche at any given moment and thus are the basis of any interaction with entities beyond the psyche, e.g., the environment. This dynamic state of the psyche might be called its mood. Heidegger has suggested a similar use of this concept. Mood is one's way of *being in* the world. Mood expresses itself in symbols through dreams and fantasies and in myths. Hence, through the study of these products, the archetypal dynamic can be determined or described.

Now to return to the category of elegance. As noted, elegance may be expressed as the tension between the dynamic of change, novelty, diversity, and the dynamic of harmony, order, simplicity. Again, it may be convincingly argued that these very principles are rooted in the human psyche and well represented by its natural symbols. The human psyche itself is, after all, a natural product of the universe and thus inherently represents the reality that we are trying to conceive. Thus, in all the criteria set forth, a metasymbol system based on the natural symbols of the psyche seems to be the key. That system rests largely on the psychological investigations of C. G. Jung. His system, however, cannot be held responsible for the application in this book. Jung would not countenance the thought that he was edging into the realm of philosophy, metaphysics, and, more particularly, theology. Nonetheless, as Paul Tillich rightly understood, Jung was laying a foundation for theology, an empirical foundation as firm as that of biology. Jung was doing the work of the theologian, but he did not push on to draw the obvious conclusions. Nonetheless, he prepared the way for a new approach to theology by creating a metasymbol system founded on the natural symbols of the human psyche. This sort of system is *the* requisite tool for any hermeneutic of human experience. Such a tool will also produce the most useful theology possible. Recall Calvin's often quoted statement about theology: "The knowledge of man and the knowledge of God are given together, and which is prior, no one can say." Calvin seems to have tried to begin with God, but it seems more proper, even necessary, to begin with ourselves lest we get lost in projections. To begin with ourselves requires beginning with the natural symbols of the psyche.

This innate, instinctual, or natural symbol system seems always to include some notion of a transcendent center that is also immanent in the individual psyche. Jung has argued and given evidence that this center, which he calls the Self, or the God-archetype, pervades and guides (through its compensatory character) the psyche in its pilgrimage. The symbols thrown into consciousness by the transpersonal psyche do not vary limitlessly or randomly but fall into patterns that represent the various archetypes and the dynamic interrelationship of archetypal forces. Because the Hero pattern seems particularly important, at least in Western civilization, it offers a means of checking the relevance of the insights that I have presented. What I have offered is, after all, a myth/symbol system in itself, even though it is an attempt at a metasymbol system. The problem is that the psyche is trying to understand itself, and as all effort to understand must be through *some* myth/symbol system, a metasymbol system is necessary. But will that system offer a transformation key by which we can better understand the developmental processes of the psyche, its structure, and its dynamics?

III

Myth, Faith, and Symbols

THE EMERGING CONSCIOUSNESS, or myth/symbol system, grows out of our better understanding of human perception and its limits. As has been noted, it was for many decades believed that the human consciousness perceived the external world directly, that it was, in fact, the work of the external world upon consciousness that prompted and directed the entire development of human intelligence. Such naïveté is no longer tenable. We always *see* the world *as;* that is, we always put upon the data of the senses a construction that shapes it into a form compatible with our shared cultural myth or our personal myths. But how does this shared cultural myth come to be? What is its history?

We may safely presume that at some time in the history of the world our primitive ancestors did not enjoy the kind of consciousness we do but instead were more akin to the animal realm in general. Perception and interpretation under such conditions are automatic, regulated by instinct. The equivalent of knowledge under such conditions is best termed "knowledge by projection." *Projection* is a psychological term meaning the attribution of some quality of the psyche to some aspect of the external world (i.e., nonpsychic world, or at least not one's own psyche). Under these conditions there is no appropriate discrimination between inner and outer. As Jean Piaget has demonstrated, the infant begins life with a sense of global unity: all things are one with the infant; there is no I-Other separation. In *Creation Myths*, M.L. von

Franz's discussion of this process is very helpful. She observes of cognition:

> When there is an original projection it means that an archetype has been constellated in the unconscious, B. The subject stares at the object, C, and can make no sense of it, but wonders what the hell it is! Then he gets an idea and conceives of the object as being so and so, but he is not aware of the fact that the archetype, B, has been constellated in his unconscious and has conveyed to him the model of the idea from which he recognizes C [the object]; he sees only that the object coincides with his idea. This is what constitutes the cognition process as a whole.[1]

Archetypes of the unconscious are attached by projection to outer objects; the outer objects then become, *unconsciously*, the symbols for the inner quality. The symbol is the means for the so-called stimulus-response pattern in humans.

The essence of Jung's discoveries about the psyche is that these projections, this pattern of symbol formation, are not merely random but are influenced by the innate structures of the psyche, the archetypes. The baby chick is born with the ability to recognize and respond by flight from the appearance of the chicken hawk, or a similar silhouette, to the security of the mother hen. The baby sea turtle, upon breaking out of the shell, moves immediately to reach the security of the nearby ocean. Baby chicks do not flee from other silhouettes or birds; baby turtles do not run away from but toward the sea. Similarly, the inner psychic archetypes are usually projected onto appropriate external factors. The earliest and most powerful projection is that of the Mother archetype upon the external mother. Among animals a similar event is called imprinting. The baby animal at a particular point projects (the mother identity) upon someone or something in its environment and from then on treats that object as mother. There are variations in this imprinting capability. Some animals will imprint only on the true mother; others will imprint on other species, including persons.

Among humans, however, the process of knowing is somewhat more complex because it is subject to further growth, development, and change, particularly the development of far greater consciousness, through which many projections are withdrawn. Because a projection is unconscious, it cannot be recognized or controlled. We are simply subject to its effects in such forms as likes, dislikes, emotional surges, and behavioral drives. Projection is most common when the object, or stimulus situation, is vague or unknown, when one does not have a developed scheme of consciousness that includes the object in a myth/symbol system. The psyche starts the process of knowing by projection, by assigning certain of its content to the observed unknown. A familiar example is the Rorschach inkblot test. The subject responds to each of the inkblot cards by telling what he or she sees. Confronted with these random blots, the psyche imposes patterns from its own structure so that one sees butterflies, trees, spiders. By projection, the previously unknown is given some identification, connected with some psychic structure. Without original projection, objects go unnoticed. An entity is made visible and sensible to consciousness by clothing it appropriately. At the outset of knowing an object, this process happens unconsciously; as long as it continues to be unconscious, the object is made to conform to some unconscious content of the subject.

Projection is not a conscious process; hence, it is neither recognized nor controlled by ego. Ego is presented with the result of projection; the incoming stimuli are construed, and we "see as." Through the processes of life, our interactions with our environment and with significant others, however, some of these projections are affirmed and others negated. Thus, by a natural process of reward and reinforcement or of negative feedback, the favorable projections are strengthened and the unfavorable ones weakened. However, as von Franz observes of a projection:

> As long as one is caught in it, as long as the archetype is validly constellated in one's unconscious and conscious, one will never call it a projection but will consider it to be true cognition. The subject then feels that he is talking about true facts as honestly as he can. . . . As long as we feel subjectively that we are not talking about projections but about the true quality of the object—a special aspect of our western mentality—then we call it the scientific truth.[2]

We may speculate that among our remote ancestors, over perhaps many, many millennia, a body of shared knowledge developed and was communicated through the forms of ritual and myth. But this communication was not yet conscious; it was instinctual. Primitive groups who live by collective projections have a low level of consciousness; their responses are mostly automatic. Levy-Bruhl called this collective response *participation mystique.* Even moderns are more subject than we realize to this unthinking collective response. Mobs, mass movements such as Nazism in Germany, and virulent anticommunist or anticapitalist groups are mostly living in participation mystique.

The content of the collective pattern of perception founded on projection is what is incorporated into a people's myth. Thus, myth is composed of symbols that represent the psychic content associated with certain images or objects. As mentioned earlier, this content always includes primary ideas about persons, nature, and God and the desired interrelationships of these. We are thus led to the conclusion that part of the inherent structure of the psyche has to do with "God." Jung indicates that the structure corresponding to this concept is Self, the archetype of God, the ultimate archetype of the psyche, its center and circumference, which pervades the whole. The Self, however, does not rule the psyche in the manner of an ancient Oriental potentate. The Self lures, suggests, entices. Because of the way it operates, the Self is easily ignored by the ego, but only to the peril of one's psychic health. Later, the question of the relationship of the Self to "God" and the God-image will be discussed. For now, simply note that these data in no way question the reality of God.

The knowledge of the functioning of symbols in the psyche is vital if one is to understand in even an elementary way the operation of the psyche, especially its religious dimension. A symbol is, first of all, a device that appeals to one or more of the senses. Most commonly, symbols are images or words. The defining characteristic of a symbol, however, is its capacity to affect the psyche, to elicit and direct psychic energy. Apart from the conscious symbol, psychic energy is released instinctively to the appropriate stimulus; the individual does no real choosing.

Even those whose consciousness is highly developed find that

their instincts may overwhelm them in moments of great stress or
stimulation. The three most common modes of this experience relate to instinctual ways of meeting the environment: fight, flight,
and sex. The primitive, or the undeveloped modern, has little pro-
tection against these instinctual processes; they can neither be
called up nor controlled when they are present. Only those who
have a conscious and appropriate symbolic repertoire can in any
measure control instinctual powers. The transformation of instinctual energy into a desired form or the control of it is achieved by
creating in the psyche an analogue, a conscious symbol, of the *object* of the instinct.[3]

In the earliest stages of human development, this process represents the beginning of culture, of organized activity. One of the
earliest of these organized activities came about by representing
certain agricultural activities with sexual analogies. Gaining the
ability to prepare the ground and plant the seed intentionally was
made possible by "seeing as" if plowing and planting were sexual
activities, hence, releasing and diverting energy from the sexual instinct. Among the Wachandi of Australia, this process takes the
form of a ritual dance performed about a hole in the ground that has
been surrounded with bushes to make it look like female genitals.
This dance has special significance as an earth-impregnating ceremony, turning the mind's attention to the earth and the activities
needed to make it fruitful.

In this way, although gradually and over many millennia,
humans came to have what is now known as *free will*. Through the
grace of symbol systems, people gained some control over instinctual energy. The conscious symbol can be used intentionally to call
up and channel psychic energy.

Dance, ritual, and many religious activities were practiced because they brought about certain results. At first, indeed for an untold period of time, these activities evoked no true self-
consciousness. They were as natural as the instincts they came to
control. But because they were repeated over and again, the mind
replayed them and contemplated them, which led to discoveries
about the objects represented. In some such manner as this,
humans progressed from magic to science, from mysterious self-

control through ceremonies to the beginnings of self-control through the intentional use of symbols. The symbol thus diverts, enables us to capture, a small portion of the natural flow of psychic energy—most of it continues the natural flow of life, the autonomic processes. From the diverted portion, organized and directed by symbols, humanity has become civilized and has developed its knowledge structure.

Symbols were never devised consciously; they were always produced out of the unconscious in revelation or intuition and in dreams or visions. Over a long time the psyche develops "typical pathways for energy flow," which are then culturally represented by typical symbols. These psychic pathways, or archetypes, are passed on by inheritance; their symbols are passed on by culture. The symbols created in the psyche are always grounded in the unconscious archetype, but their overt forms, the archetypal images, are shaped by the experiences and ideas of the conscious mind. "The archetypes are the numinous, structural elements of the psyche and possess a certain autonomy and specific energy which enables them to attract, out of the conscious mind, those contents which are best suited to themselves."[4]

Each stage of human development is characterized by its connection and relationship to one or more archetypal elements. In mythology the archetypes are symbolized in classic ways, i.e., in ways that are universal to the human species. Of course, symbols vary from one culture to another, but once the referent of the symbol is recognized, the variations can be seen as just that—variations on a theme. "In the course of its ontogenetic development, the individual ego consciousness has to pass through the same archetypal stages which determined the evolution of consciousness in the life of humanity. . . . As organs of the psyche's structure the archetypes articulate with one another autonomously, like the physical organs, and determine the maturation of the personality in a manner analogous to the biological hormone-components of the physical constitution."[5]

Symbols are the primary tool for controlling the instincts and building the spiritual life. Organized religions present a symbol system that functions as a counterpole to the primitive instinctual nature. Consequently, religion and culture go hand in hand. Religion is the means for the development of culture and for the development of the individual. However, "wherever the cultural process is moving forward, whether in single individuals or in groups, we find a shaking off of collective beliefs."[6] Any advance in spirituality begins with an individual, one who is conscious of isolation from the collective beliefs, one who dares to find a new pathway to unknown territory. Classically, these figures are religious Heroes, such as Abraham, Moses, Ruth, Buddha, Jesus, and Mohammed, to name only a few. To carry out such an action, Heroes must first return to the fundamental facts of their own beings, which means transcending the customary ways of understanding and acting, shaking off the blinders of tradition and custom, becoming conscious of the uniqueness of oneself. The Hero is not a product of the collective. The Hero's faith, or understanding, though doubtless conditioned by the collective beliefs, the symbol system of culture, is founded squarely upon personal life experience. Successfully gaining collective validation for the widened perspective creates in the culture a tension that is necessary for its further progress.

The new Hero or Heroine and his or her mode of consciousness then become the basis for a new collective faith, a new symbol system. As an archetypal figure, i.e., a structural aspect of every psyche, the Hero symbolizes the nature and goal of psychic energy as it inherently presses forward to greater consciousness and wholeness. The Hero is supreme among the symbols of the psyche that represent the goal of psychic energy. Western civilization has had as its supreme Hero image the Jesus of the Gospels. For nearly two thousand years this figure has recurrently gripped and shaped the imagination of the West. If we are to understand the psyche of Western peoples, we must consider carefully the Hero story, which is so fundamental to Western history and development. But we must also be cautious to note that we are dealing with archetypal symbols, not merely historical or personal data. The Hero becomes a hero by living out an archetypal pattern that is recognized, although usually unconsciously, by the followers. The Hero symbolizes in person and in ideas the forms, forces, and concepts that grip and mold the very soul, the archetypal contents of the psyche. Through the Hero, people are brought into contact with the foundations of humanity in the depths of the psyche. This contact is always a numinous experience, hence the religious nature of Heroes.

Heroes of this type never write their own autobiographies; they seldom write anything at all. Their lives are consumed in the living. Because they are archetypal, their followers, in attempting to tell about them must resort to archetypal imagery. The archetypes, however, are part of the universal collective structure of the psyche, and though the images of the archetypes vary, the referents of the images have a recognizable identity. It is not surprising, then, that the stories of Heroes, whether told by an Eskimo shaman, an Australian aborigine, or a Gospel writer, have more than a similarity of pattern. The archetypes manifest in the Hero "are precisely those that have inspired, throughout the annals of human culture, the basic images of ritual, mythology, and vision."[7] To know the Hero story is to know something of one's own psyche.

IV

The Centrality
of the Hero

MYTH is the foundation of human knowing and of all the religious and social structures we create.

> Throughout the inhabited world, in all times and under every circumstance, the myths of man have flourished; and they have been the living inspiration of whatever else may have appeared out of the activities of the human body and mind. It would not be too much to say that myth is the secret opening through which the inexhaustible energies of the cosmos pour into human cultural manifestation. Religions, philosophies, arts, the social forms of primitive and historic man, prime discoveries in science and technology, the very dreams that blister sleep, boil up from the basic, magic ring of myth.[1]

Myth lies at the root of human culture, but what is the source of myth itself?

> Since the root-ideas of myth are at a deep and basic level of consciousness, they are not always expressed in day-to-day, casual descriptions, but when a person sinks into an imaginative reverie to write a book, or to synthesize the factual results of research, then he or she is likely to move into a more mythopoeic form of narrative, for even science can be a form of story-telling.[2]

In religion the traditional answer has been *revelation*, meaning that the source and usually the content were presumed to be divine. Practically speaking, historically speaking, revelation comes in the forms of visions, dreams, fantasies, and other ecstatic experiences.

Consider, for example, Moses and the bush that burned but was not consumed—clearly a visionary experience. Isaiah in the temple (Isa. 6) had a vision of the "Lord sitting upon a throne, high and lifted up," accompanied by a tremendous sense of his own unworthiness, but followed by a call to minister to his people. Ezekiel's visions, Paul on the road to Damascus, and John on Patmos—again and again in Holy Writ we are led to these ecstatic, mystical, religious visions as the foundation of religious convictions expressed in myth. Wherever or however it occurs, myth is not made up in some conscious way; it happens spontaneously in the psyche. This is not to imply that there are no outward conditions or accompaniments but to make clear that the outward event is "seen as" by being clothed with material from the psyche. For example, whatever the experience of the people who participated in the Exodus of the Hebrews, the story as it is told in Scripture has been clothed by the mythic imagination. The story was given to us in the revelation of archetypal fantasy. Much, if not all, remembered and written history comes to us through such process, although clearly not all or even much deserves to be called inspired. "Each reporter's interpretation weaves its own myth of meaning in and out of the warp of facts,"[3] whether we are speaking of history, religion, or science.

When something happens, it may or may not, then or later, seem meaningful. If it seems promising of meaning, it becomes a subject for reflection: What is its meaning? But to ask about its meaning is to ask how it relates to the past or the future or how it illuminates the human situation. Events may thus become an example of a mythic insight, that is, this bit of experience illustrates that myth; or a bit of experience may be seen as a model insight, an instance of itself, transparent (mythical) to the meaning it bears. In the latter case, the story of the event is shaped by our innate mythmaking capacity into a mythic account that can then serve as a clue to meaning for the future. A myth says that its content is ultimately what the human story is all about.

Finally, because the psychic makeup is universal (all humans share a common archetypal structure of the psyche, as we share physical structure of the body), the myths of the world tell a universal story in a bewildering variety of costumes. It is the *same* story everywhere because it is the story of the psyche, its development, purpose, and goal. Beneath the varieties of costume, mythology is everywhere the story of the pilgrimage of psyche and the perils of the journey to which all are called but which few seem to complete.

Myth and our perception of events are intertwined in the same fashion as are theory and fact (data), or subjectivity and objectivity. In observing data, we are guided by intuition and theory, e.g., in deciding what to observe, how to observe, which data to record. Our reporting is inevitably cast in language that reflects some theoretical assumptions. Choosing between the two poles of language and among the intermediate forms on the continuum implies or states a position that has already been guided by assumptions about the data.

Historical data, or personal experiences, are always viewed through some myth, even though the new data may be suggesting a new way of viewing, a new myth. Our experience in the creation of twentieth century science has been one of acquiring new data, which then required a new myth. Mythic symbols are the clothing that give meaning to otherwise barren happenings. The poet viewing the lion experiences a flow of mythic images and so describes the lion. "King of the jungle," "fearful symmetry," "claws like rapiers," "a roar like thunder"—all these describe more the inner experience of the poet than the objective life of the lion. It is an easy step from sentiments like these to using the lion himself as a symbol for kings, fearful power, for clever hunting. This imagery is then woven into a story base and becomes part of the fabric of the culture, perhaps in this case a totem.

The form of myth that is to be investigated here is the Hero myth, particularly as exemplified in the Gospel stories about Jesus. Erich Neumann has demonstrated, in his monumental work, *The Origins and History of Consciousness*, that the Hero is the archetypal forerunner of humankind in general and that the stages of the Hero myth have become constituent elements in the personal development of every individual. The individual human psyche, in the course of its development, must pass through the same archetypal stages that have governed the evolution of consciousness in

the life of humanity. The Hero exemplifies that course of development. Neumann has also shown that a series of archetypes, i.e.,
typical structures of the psyche, are the main constituents of mythology and that these represent definite stages of development. As
he notes, "Ego consciousness evolves by passing through a series of
'eternal images,' and the ego, transformed in the passage, is con-
stantly experiencing a new relation to the archetypes. Its relationship to the eternality of the archetypal images is a process of
succession in time—that is to say, it takes place in stages."[4] As Neumann goes on to note, the various archetypes that determine development make up only a small portion of the whole of archetypal
reality. The extent of archetypal reality is unknowably vast and
seems best connected with Alfred North Whitehead's notions of
"eternal objects" or the Platonic "ideas," i.e., all the potentials of
the universe, realized and unrealized.

For the human, development proceeds, then, in stages that
are related to certain transpersonal, or universal, psychic factors.
Further, these transpersonal factors are not external conditions of
society to which individuals must conform but are internal structural elements.[5] Just as a typical life-span includes birth, childhood, adolescence, maturity, and death, so do comparable
psychological structures typically shape all growth. The individual
embroiders a personal pattern upon this structural frame, but all
people develop by a common pathway of stages in the psyche. As
is true of physical growth, not all persons develop at the same
rate, nor do all reach the same fullness of development. This difference is especially important as we look down the evolutionary
ladder. "The individualized conscious man of our era is a late
man, whose structure is built on early, pre-individual human
stages from which individual consciousness has only detached itself step by step."[6] Thus, in interpreting ancient documents, the
"average" stage of psychic development must be considered in
terms of the audience, the individual stage in terms of the author
or protagonists. This pattern of stage-by-stage development,
which is related to the internal, collective, structural, and archetypal forces, is the central story of the human situation. It is the
archetypal factors that "cause" development in the individual's

life, not the external factors of family or society. The external factors follow the stages of development and depend upon them, not vice versa. For example, just as we do not look for the causes of puberty in the environment, neither should we look for the causes of adolescence in the psyche. The environment is certainly not passive; it may assist, cooperate with, or hinder psychic development. Environment, culture, its dominant myths and consequent behavioral patterns are critical considerations in psychic development, but the germ, the triggering and guiding forces, comes from the transpersonal psyche. Nonetheless, the developing ego is strongly affected and shaped by cultural forces.

Neumann has worked with the broad spectrum of the mythological canon in his study of development, and Campbell has worked with all the aspects of the world mythology relating to the Hero.[7] In the following chapters I will discuss only the Hero myth as exemplified in the Gospel stories of Jesus. The first reason is that, as noted earlier, this Hero story is the model story for Western civilization. Certainly, the writings of Dante, Shakespeare, and Milton were strongly influenced by the Hero theme. The Hero pattern lies at the very root of our culture and is still being retold in Western literature and cinema, detective stories, science-fiction thrillers (e.g. *Star Wars*) and comic books. Creation myths belong to the first cycle of development, the origins of consciousness from its embryonic state in the unconscious up to the beginnings of true consciousness. In an infant's life this stage might be loosely equated to the period before the onset of language capability. The Hero cycle of myth belongs to the second and, to this point in history, most important phase of human psychic development. The Hero myth takes us from the birth of consciousness, through its full development, including the detachment of ego from the transpersonal center and to its reconnection through the mysteries of the mythic *hieros gamos*, the marriage of the personal and the transpersonal, the transcendence of simple sexual identity in androgyny, and so to apotheosis. The personal develops out of the transpersonal and is dependent upon it, although part of the ego's task of development is to detach itself from the transpersonal center, the Self. But this detachment is not the end of development, for the ego remains rooted in the transpersonal center, and for its final and supreme stage of development must be reunited with that center in a new identity and relation. So the second reason for considering the Hero myth as exemplified in Jesus is that it represents our own individual development; that is, its symbols are those of our psyches. In sum, the Hero is the archetypal forerunner of humanity in general, but the particular form that the Hero story has taken in the West is exemplified in the story of Jesus. However much we miss or fall short of this idea, "the stages of the hero myth have become constituent elements in the personal development of every individual."[8] That is, every person is called to the Hero pilgrimage, the spiritual journey: that pilgrimage is the primary, perhaps the only, purpose of life. As we shall see, we are not called to imitate or duplicate some earlier Hero, but each of us is to make a Hero journey, which, though it passes through the same stages, is unlike any other Hero journey.

V

The Hero's Birth Story

A COMPARISON of the Jesus story with that of other world mythological heroes discloses a remarkable similarity of pattern. This equivalency of pattern, the fact that the Gospels were written at least sixty years after the birth of Jesus, and what we know of the Gospel writers' art, lead to the conclusion that the birth story of Jesus is a mythically shaped account, not a biographical account. This story was probably created in bits and pieces by pious speculation about Jesus' early life and summed up in a masterwork by Luke, the Gospel writer.[1]

Luke saw Jesus' life pattern as a recapitulation of the Genesis pattern, the book of beginnings. Matthew followed a similar method, but the motif for him was Jesus as the fulfillment of the law. Both saw Jesus against the background of the messianic hopes of the people, for, Heroes come in a time of great need, a time of spiritual and social poverty and unrest. In late Judaism, the messianic hope prominently included the notions that Messiah would be (1) the son of David; (2) born at Bethlehem, David's birthplace and ancestral home; and (3) born of a virgin.

Briffault has demonstrated the worldwide belief in the virgin birth of the Hero, whether in North or South American, Polynesian, Asian, European, or African myth.[2] In the ancient world, however, virginity was not a sexual state but a state of spiritual independence. A virgin did not belong to any man but was her own person. Virginity was regarded as sacred, not because it was a state of physical purity, but because it was a psychic purity of openness to God and God alone. The Hero's mother is thus identified with the female deity, the Mother Goddess, or archetypically, the Great Mother. Originally, in mythology, the Great Mother Goddess was the only true creator; later, she has a divine consort who is responsible for her impregnation. A procreative masculine element, which is represented by the Holy Ghost in Jesus' story, is at work in the Mother.

All archetypes are bipolar, as is the universe itself. To those of us in the West, the bipolarity of the universe is less clear than the bipolarity of language because we have been nurtured in a monopolar, or dichotomized, view. Part of the story of our civilization has been an attempt to divide the world into "common and preferred" and then to grasp only the preferred. We have tended to believe that light can be had without dark, that good is separable from evil; we have broken apart spirit and matter, mind and body, the temporal and eternal, *ad infinitum*. The general method, which can be traced as far back as the Greeks, is to take each pair of ultimate contraries (e.g., one and many, permanence and change, necessity and contingency), decide which member is desired or admirable, and then attribute to it ultimate excellency, finally lodging it in deity itself.[3]

A different way of viewing the world has become necessary in science and philosophy: that way may be expressed as the law of polarity. "According to this law, ultimate contraries are correlatives, mutually interdependent, so that nothing real can be described by the wholly one-sided assertion of simplicity, being, actuality, and the like, each in a 'pure' form, devoid and independent of complexity, becoming, potentiality, and related contraries."[4] This same law of polarity is observed in mythic and archetypal structures or figures, which accords with our scientific and philosophical knowledge about reality. Much, if not most, theology of the West has presumed the monopolar view, attributing the chosen superior pole to God and his work, relegating the other to evil, or the devil and his work. This invidious dichotomizing and favoritism is easily illustrated in the current debate over women's liberation. Our culture has traditionally attributed to woman infe-

mate ?

rior traits that make her suited only to be man's helpmeet, never
his equal. For example, she has been considered passive, weak,
unintellectual, uncreative, unstable, emotional; by contrast, a man
has been considered the embodiment of the opposite characteristics, which are, of course, the good ones. Current research has
thoroughly exploded the validity of any such categorizing.

Like all archetypes, the Great Mother has a light and a dark
side. To understand her dark side, we must first realize the Hero's
mission and its relationship to his own nature. The Hero's destiny
is, first, the separation of ego-consciousness from the matriarchal
bed of instinctuality, the rule of the unconscious. The Hero leads
the way to conscious individuality and responsibility. This means
the overcoming of all the demons and instinctual drives of the
psyche through the establishment of an appropriate ego-conscious
center. Second, the Hero must overcome the external enemies—
the forces that fight against change and for the status quo. These
forces are found both in the archetypes and in their social representatives. The dark side of the Great Mother appears as the possessive mother and, in another form, as the repressive society.
Mythologically, this dark aspect is often presented as the dragon,
which the Hero must overcome. The light side, or aspect, of the
Great Mother is her capacity to nurture and inspire. She is the
container or the seedbed in which life begins and by which it is
nurtured and protected until it can be more independent. In this
respect, the Virgin Mary symbolizes the nurturing Great Mother.
Sophia, the wisdom and compassion of the Father God of the Old
Testament, is a symbol of the inspiring aspect of the Great
Mother.[5] However, in myth, masculinity is associated with light
and consciousness, femininity with darkness and unconsciousness;
thus, both the Hero and his accomplishments are masculinized.
Nonetheless, a patriarchal society may come to be the servant of
the dark aspect of the Great Mother archetype, the dragon, which
opposes the Hero.

So, as the creed has it, Jesus is conceived by the Holy Ghost
and born of the Virgin Mary. At the outset of this story, we see only
the good aspect of the mother, pure and undefiled, and she is presented in a context that demonstrates her appropriateness to be the

Mother of God. As noted earlier, Luke's inspiration appears to have
been the Genesis pattern. The central character of Genesis is Jacob
(Israel), who, according to Jewish tradition, was the father of twelve
sons, each of whom was destined to be the patriarch of a tribe.
Jesus has twelve disciples and Paul, then, refers to the church as
the "new Israel." The main plot of Genesis, after its mythic foundations in Genesis 1—11:9, centers on Abraham (who may be called
the first hero of consciousness), and then includes his sons, Isaac
and Jacob. Luke picks up this story line by showing Jesus as a continuation of the line of prophecy and fulfillment; that is, in Jesus, a
new chain of prophecy begins as God's Spirit is released anew in
him.[6]

In building his story, Luke models the father and the mother of
John the Baptist on Abraham and Sarah. John's mother, Elizabeth,
is old and barren, like Sarah. John's father, Zacharias, like Abraham, is also advanced in years and is warned of the coming birth
with the formula that was used to tell Abraham, "Your wife Elizabeth will bear you a son, and you shall call his name . . ." (Luke:
1:13). Like Abraham, he disbelieves, naturally using Abraham's
words of doubt, "How shall I know this?" (Luke 1:18).

Whether or not John the Baptist's father was, in fact, the priest
Zacharias is unknown. What is obvious, however, is that there are
some very good reasons for using the name. John stands in the line
of the martyr prophets. The Old Testament ends with a foretelling
of a successor to Elijah: "Behold, I send my messenger to prepare
the way before me, and the Lord whom you seek will suddenly
come to his temple . . ." (Mal. 3:1). "Behold, I will send you Elijah
the prophet before the great and terrible day of the LORD comes"
(Mal. 4:5). John is clearly Luke's presentation of Elijah's preparing
the way.

Part of the wonder of Hero births is that many of them are foretold by divine portents or angelic warnings. For such a birth as this,
who would be the appropriate angel? In the Old Testament an angel foretold the Christ. Gabriel, in Daniel 9:20, and an angel whom
Daniel encounters later provide the form for Gabriel's meeting
with Zachariah. In each instance the angel is not seen by others;
both men are afraid and are reassured with the words "Fear not!"

Both then hear the prophecy and are immediately struck dumb. The words of this prophecy are modeled upon the words of another angel, who announced the birth of Samson (Judg. 13:2–5, 24).

The story now turns to Jesus. The annunciation of Jesus' birth exactly parallels that of John's birth, but for the content of the announcement, Luke turned to Isaiah, the major prophet of the incarnation, and to the first annointed one, David. In the Septuagint, Isaiah 7:14 and 9:6–7 promise a Messiah who will be born to a virgin and who will establish his ideal government on the throne of David. This fits in beautifully with the promises made to David and to his son in 2 Samuel 7:8–17, culminating in "your kingdom shall be made sure . . . ; your throne shall be established forever."

The model for Mary is provided by the ideal mother of the Old Testament, Hannah, mother of Samuel. So, just as Hannah described herself as the handmaid of the Lord and rejoiced over her son with a poetic hymn, so does Mary, in words very much like those of Hannah. Compare the words of Hannah in 1 Samuel 2:1–10 with those of Mary in Luke 1:46–55.

Because Micah 5:2 had dictated that the appropriate birthplace would be Bethlehem, Luke devised a clever reason to have the holy family go there from Joseph's town of Nazareth. Matthew had given no reason, but Luke knew of the census ordered in A.D. 9 by Quirinius and used that as a device to get the family out of Galilee, which was no place for the Messiah to be born.

Naturally, an event as important as the birth of the Messiah must have heavenly recognition—Heroes always do. The words used are those implied in Isaiah 6:3 and 57:19, "Glory to God in the highest and on earth peace among men with whom he is pleased."

The closing episode is the presentation of Jesus in the temple by Mary, just as Hannah, her prototype, had presented Samuel in the temple at Shiloh. Both families then returned to the provinces, and both boys grew in stature and in favor with the Lord.

Matthew tells us of the Wise Men who came from the East, following the star. The birth of a divine universal Hero is no small thing; the very foundations of the creation are shaken. And such a birth is not for Jews alone; Gentiles, too, wait in darkness for a savior. Certainly, their wise men would be aware of this birth, just as would the simple Jewish peasants who abided in the fields by night. Isaiah, Chapter 60, provides the needed inspiration: "And nations shall come to your light, and kings to the brightness of your rising" (vs. 3). But it also must be noted that the Gentiles (Babylonians?) were followers of astrology and would have known that an unusual conjunction was taking place; at least their wise men would have known. Seen in the context of astrological myth, Jesus' birth marks the end of one astrological era and the beginning of the next. As Jung noted, although no connection can be proved between the figure of Christ and the inception of the astrological age of Pisces (the fishes),

> it would be clear to anyone acquainted with astrology that he was born as the first fish of the Pisces era, and was doomed to die as the last ram [*arnion*, lamb] of the declining Aries era. . . . As a zodiacal sign, therefore, it is not in the least remarkable. It becomes a matter for astonishment only when, through the precession of the equinoxes, the spring-point moves into this sign and thus inaugurates an age in which the "fish" was used as a name for the God who became a man, who was born as a fish and was sacrificed as a ram, who had fishermen for disciples and wanted to make them fishers of men, who fed the multitude with miraculously multiplying fishes, who was himself eaten as a fish, the "holier food", and whose followers are little fishes, the "pisciculi".[7]

Christ was often referred to in the early Church with the Greek word/acronym, IXΘΥΣ (*ichthus*, "fish"), which meant Jesus Christ, Son of God, Savior.

The story of Jesus' birth is not limited to the Gospel accounts. In its development, the Church meditated upon this material and upon its own inner experience of the Hero, and the canon of myth was extended. The seasons and symbols of the Christian year, as expressed in liturgy, are the result. Around the birth of the Hero there grew up a seasonal celebration—Advent, Christmas, and Epiphany. The Hero is thus identified as light, the sun, the "Light of the World," the daystar. Symbolically, that is, in the natural symbols of the psyche as found in myth, light is equated with consciousness. Darkness is equated with unconsciousness and with instinctual drivenness. For thousands of years before Jesus' birth, pre-Christian symbols and ritual celebrated the midwinter solstice, the beginning of the return of the sun. The sun was not just a source of light and warmth but was a symbol for that inner source of light within the psyche.

For primitive peoples, those who have not advanced to high levels of ego-conscious development, consciousness, and its consequent control over instinctual drives, is somewhat precarious. When not actively driven to think by outward circumstances, primitives usually go to sleep, as do animals. They also experience loss of control of consciousness more easily than is customary in us; this loss of control is often described as loss of soul. Have you not sometimes found yourself drowsing over a book that you wanted to read with care? That is an experience of consciousness, the light, slipping away. For primitives, this loss of light was a constant possibility and was very much feared; hence, the light was celebrated. The Hero figure is the champion of consciousness; consequently, he is associated with the light and the sun. Naturally, the birthday of the Hero is the same as the birthday of the sun, the midwinter solstice.

So it is to be expected, it is appropriate symbolically, that the beginning of the Christian year coincides with the period when humans, from time immemorial, have celebrated the birth of the sun. This, symbolically, is the midnight of the year, and according to tradition, that is, mythic legend, Jesus was born at midnight on the winter solstice.

Advent, which is a preparation for Christmas, begins with our remembering the world of darkness before the Hero—Christ— came. From the Christian perspective, Israel remained in darkness, captive to the power of Satan, trapped in a fallen universe, i.e., enslaved to the Mother Dragon of the psyche, the unconscious. So, the traditional prayer of Advent:

> O Day-Spring, Brightness of the light eternal
> And Sun of Justice, come and enlighten those who
> Sit in darkness and the shadow of death.

Or again, we sing,

> O come, O come Emmanuel,
> And ransom captive Israel,
> That mourns in lonely exile here.

It was also observed that at the birth of the sun-hero, which occurs annually at the winter solstice, a particular constellation is always rising in the east. The name assigned to the constellation is Virgo, the virgin, and the image of that constellation is a woman holding a shock of wheat. She is the mother of the sun-hero.

VI

The Meaning of the Birth of the Hero

A BASIC FACT of myth seems to be that consciousness is symbolized as masculine; also, it is apparent throughout patriarchal cultures that the masculine has been identified with consciousness and its growth. The unconscious, by contrast, is symbolized as maternal and feminine. Consciousness is born from the Mother unconscious. "The phases in the development of consciousness appear then as embryonic containment in the mother, as childlike dependence on the mother, as the relation of the beloved son to the Great Mother, and finally as the heroic struggle of the male hero against the Great Mother."[1] Not only men undergo this struggle against the negative, containing forces of the unconscious. Woman also experiences the development of consciousness, so this, too, is her struggle, and the Hero symbolizes her development of consciousness. The Great Mother of myth has a dual symbolism—light-dark, life-death, nurturing-destroying. The Great Mother gives and takes away, from dust to dust.

> The unconscious has a Janus-face: on one side its contents point back to a pre-conscious, prehistoric world of instinct, while on the other side it potentially anticipates the future—precisely because of the instinctive readiness for action of the factors that determine man's fate.[2]

Ego, the "I," the center of consciousness, begins as a germ or an embryo contained in the Mother unconscious. Not until about the end of the first year does ego begin to manifest itself in consciousness as the center of an awareness of a differentiation between inner and outer, between I and other, the "other" at first being one's own body. Only at about age three is there enough ego development and ego-awareness that the use of the first-person pronoun begins. The ego is now becoming an agent of will and a center of consciousness, the latter having functioned as an acting center to respond to instinctual forces and do their bidding. The ego is emancipating itself from the overriding power of the unconscious. The story of the Hero is the story of ego from the onset of consciousness to its far-off goal of apotheosis. The same psychic forces that foster development in the psyche are responsible for the creation of culture, i.e., civilization, particularly in the form of stable patterns as found in law, social order, and social mores. These forces are in general symbolized as heaven. The focus is on the development of an ego-consciousness that is capable of self-control in the face of the demands of instinct. In myth, instinctual forces are symbolically associated with the feminine, the world of the Great Mother.

This first transformation interrupts, or breaks apart, the seamless unity of experience in which the infant, the mother and the father, and the whole environment are one. The preconscious infant lives in an undifferentiated continuum of experience, a primal unity of child-parent-world. It is the memory of this precious bliss that later becomes a sense of paradise lost and a permanent longing for eternity. Hence, the first emergence of the Hero archetype is not only to be associated with the coming of ego-consciousness but is also connected with that profound sense of loss that is called the fall, or paradise lost. This sense of loss is also sometimes referred to as a "God-shaped blank" in the heart of man, an emptiness that gnaws until it finds respite in God.

At the same time, as the New Testament properly teaches, the birth of the Hero is divine and is to be celebrated, not mourned or regretted. Adam's fall is that "blessed sin" that calls forth "so great a salvation." Transformation, in this case the emergence of ego-consciousness, is always a divine process to be celebrated rather than mourned, but always it means a loss also of the earlier organization. In the emergence of ego the loss is great indeed—gone is primal bliss. But the gain is also immeasurable; a new reality, ego-consciousness, has come from the Creator of all things. "The separation of the son from the Mother signifies man's leave-taking from animal unconsciousness."[3] This step is, beyond the creation of the psyche itself, one of the greatest developments in evolutionary history. Alfred North Whitehead speaks of the child's discovery of the principle of symbolism in language as one of the greatest feats of learning in life. He also notes that the purpose of symbolism is the furtherance of life's demand for freedom and self-creativity. "In the place of the force of instinct which suppresses individuality, society has gained the efficacy of symbols, at once preservative of the commonweal and of the individual standpoint. . . . The symbolic expression of instinctive forces drags them out into the open; it differentiates them and delineates them. There is then opportunity for reason to effect, with comparative speed, what otherwise must be left to the slow operation of the centuries amid ruin and reconstruction."[4]

In the birth of the Hero, it is clear that God is doing a "new thing." That is why, in the myths, the Hero is always born of a virgin, and either the father or the mother, or both, are divine. The miraculous birth represents the understanding of the miraculous quality of this development of the psyche. Transformation to a higher level of psychic development, here the birth of ego-consciousness, is never an achievement of humanity; rather, it happens to us, as though by some outside agent. The development may be heralded in various ways, it may be devoutly sought and prayed for, but when it occurs it does so as a gift whose author seems divine.

Although divine and religiously sought, the new birth is regarded with suspicion, anxiety, and even outright fear. The numinous is always frightening as well as fascinating. Because it is the basis of a new cultural as well as individual development, the birth of the Hero is an occasion for cultural and personal unrest. This unrest has two foundations. For the culture and the individual, the emergence of the truly new signifies the death of an old pattern. When the child, for example, develops an ego, life is never again the same for the mother, either. "A new element in life renders in many ways the operation of the old instincts unsuitable." Even novelties that involve a rise to finer levels of life have this disruptive tendency and are thus regarded at best with suspicion and at worst with murderous hatred. "It is the first step in sociological wisdom, to recognize that the major advances in civilization are processes which all but wreck the societies in which they occur."[5] Hence, in myth, the ruling tyrant knows that the newly born Hero is a living threat to his reign and sends out orders to seek and destroy all new-born male children. Novelty is always met with suspicion by those forces who most benefit by the status quo both in culture and in psyche. The children of the Great Mother are intended to be her servants, not individuals.

The second foundation of unrest is the precariousness of a new development. Just as a newborn infant is fragile, delicate, easily de-stroyed, so is a newly born psychic development. The sheer inertia of the instinctual psyche is extremely difficult to overcome so that a new process can be set in motion. "The motifs of 'insignificance,' exposure, abandonment, danger, try to show how precarious is the psychic possibility . . . the enormous difficulties to be met with in attaining this 'highest good.' "[6] Jung described these difficulties, which will beset the developing psyche in its whole passage through life, in a superb paragraph:

> . . . in the morning of life the son tears himself loose from the mother. . . . Always he imagines his worst enemy in front of him, yet he carries the enemy within himself—a deadly longing for the abyss, a longing to drown in his own source, to be sucked down to the realm of the Mothers. . . . This death is no external enemy, it is his own inner longing for the stillness and profound peace of all-knowing non-exis-tence, for all-seeing sleep in the ocean of coming-to-be and passing away. . . . If he is to live, he must fight and sacrifice his longing for the past in order to rise to his own heights.[7]

It is necessary, even at the birth of the Hero, to begin to take notice of his dual character. As an archetype the Hero is un-separated from the instinctual psyche. Because all archetypal ele-ments share this characteristic, they, like the Great Mother, who symbolizes the instinctual psyche, the unconscious, are bipolar rather than monopolar entities. Each has a side that favors light, life, development, and process and a side that favors darkness, death, regression, or status quo. The Hero, too, has a dark, shadow side, which is an ally of the Great and Terrible Mother. In Christian history this shadow side of the Hero has been called the antiChrist, or the devil, Satan, the tempter. The Hero faces the enemy without—the dragon forces of the tyrant society and its king—but also the dragon forces within, which would draw the Hero back into unconsciousness, the realm of instinct. Jung noted that the Hero who clings to the mother is the dragon; only when he is born away from the mother, in a rebirth, can he become the conquerer of the dragon.[8]

Purely psychologically, the Hero represents the positive, favorable action of the unconscious; the dragon is its negative and unfavorable action (i.e., greedy retention and devouring) rather than rebirth and transformation. This duality is necessary also because the Hero signifies, psychologically, the Self, that central archetype of the whole psyche. The Self is a true *coincidentia oppositorum*, which must simultaneously contain light and dark because it represents and encompasses the whole psyche. Our modern rationalistic tendency, present in Christianity from its early days, has led us to do away with this dark aspect of the Hero and of the Self as part of our splitting the world into opposites, shunned and preferred. We banish these dragon-devil forces by claiming that they are only illusions or that they belong to some dark sinister force outside the psyche (although they can invade it). The positivist seems to regard them as superstitions left behind from the age of magic and myth. The reality of this dark side is evidenced, however, by every crime, every war, every neurotic attempt to escape from the growth demanded by life. Not everyone who is gripped by the Hero image takes the path of sainthood; a negative identification can produce an Adolph Hitler, a Charles Manson, or a juvenile mugger whose favorite targets are the old and the helpless.

Yet always, even in the darkness of negative identification with the dark side of the Hero, the Hero figures of human history stand out against the masses of humanity who live merely conventional lives.

> Their greatness has never lain in their abject submission to convention, but, on the contrary, in their deliverance *from* convention. They tow-

ered up like mountain peaks above the mass that still clung to its collective fears, its beliefs, laws, and systems, and boldly chose their own way. To the man in the street it has always seemed miraculous that anyone should turn aside from the beaten track with its known destinations, and strike out on the steep and narrow path leading into the unknown. Hence it was always believed that such a man, if not actually crazy, was possessed by a daemon or a god; for the miracle of a man being able to act otherwise than as humanity has always acted could only be explained by the gift of a daemonic power or a divine spirit. . . . From the beginning, therefore, the heroes were endowed with godlike attributes.[9]

As I will describe in more detail later, our relationship to the Hero archetype can develop properly only if we incorporate and reconcile the polarities, light and dark, of the psyche. The relationship does not work if we identify with one pole and cast the other into infernal darkness. Those who identify with the light are always in danger from the repressed dark side, and repression reinforced by divine identification (that is, identification with the all-white Hero), can produce an immense shadow. Those who identify with the dark side, on the other hand, simply live out the shadow forces, always the tool of their own instincts until their tiny original candle of life is snuffed out in the damp cave of unconsciousness, leaving the dragon triumphant. Wholeness, i.e., soundness, health, is not simply identification or fusion with either pole but the inclusion of polarity within a higher union symbolized by the mythic Hero's dragon-conquering ability. "We need both poles to understand either one because each is involved in the development and completion of the other."[10]

VII

Departure and Initiation

CAMPBELL OBSERVED that the Hero journey proper begins with "the call to adventure." This call may be something so small that it goes unnoticed, a blunder or mere chance, but it is a herald. The reasoning is that Jesus' story as told in the Gospels is perceived by virtue of the Hero archetype and hence will reveal patterns essentially like those of the worldwide Hero myths. The role of herald is apparently filled by John the Baptist, and the call to adventure by the incident of Jesus' baptism. In the Hero myth patterns "the call rings up the curtain, always, on a mystery of transfiguration—a rite, or moment, of spiritual passage, which, when complete, amounts to a dying and a birth. The familiar life horizon has been outgrown; the old concepts, ideals, and emotional patterns no longer fit; the time for the passing of a threshold is at hand."[1]

In the myths generally, the herald is a creature representing the simpler levels of animal development, e.g., a toad or frog, or some sort of loathsome monster. This is the representation because the call to adventure is a call to begin the battle to control the forces of instinct, to bring the forces to consciousness. In the symbolic economy of the psyche these instinctual forces are usually represented by some lowly animal form. Many of these instinctual forces are known by us but are repressed, forced out of consciousness and into the depths. There they form, as it were, a shadow pool of dark potential. Here we hoard the repressed, rejected, unadmitted, unrecognized, unwanted potentials of our existence. Jung called the zone of the psyche that holds these possibilities the personal unconscious; the psychic figure that represents these possibilities he called the Shadow. The personal unconscious contains other materials also, everything that constitutes one's life history but that has disappeared from consciousness. The Shadow is a mediatorial figure in this context, relating the ego to the personal unconscious. Jung used the name Shadow to personify "those contents in ourselves that we repress because they are unacceptable, such as tawdry thoughts, unbounded power aspirations, secret faults."[2] He indicated that the Shadow is the first figure we meet on the road to mature psychic development. Usually, the Shadow is met first in projection; one's own dark side is met as though it really belonged to another. A first task of the maturing psyche is to withdraw such projections by getting to know its own Shadow.

In psychic development each transition from one stage of life to the next may be called a transformation. Every transformation is, in effect, a death and a rebirth because transformation means putting aside a settled or established pattern of life and taking up a new pattern, dying to the old to be born again to the new. For the Hero the most important transformation is his *vocatio*, his call, to be a Hero, and his initiation, which establishes that *vocatio*. It is thus fitting that the transformation of *vocatio* be lifted up as a death and rebirth experience. In Christian thought, baptism is viewed as a death and a rebirth. The Apostle Paul refers to this understanding as he writes to the Colossians: "you were buried with him in baptism, in which you were also raised with him" (Col.2:12). Paul also alludes to this death-rebirth experience and connects it with the overcoming of instinctual forces: "If with Christ you died to the elemental spirits of the universe, why do you live as if you still belonged to the world?" (Col. 2:20).[3]

Transformation in antiquity was always viewed as a gift of the gods, a mystery that passes understanding. It was a source of wonder to the average person that anyone could act contrary to the established modes. In our day of highly independent ego development, it is no cause for wonder when someone acts independently, but for a society that lived in almost total collectivity, whose life patterns were

molded firmly by tradition, an independent act or thought was aston-
ishing and required the intervention of deity. Because heroes are the
embodiment of "God's new thing," they are always viewed as instru-
ments or embodiments of divinity. "Man is not merely born in the
commonplace sense, but is born again in a mysterious manner, and
so partakes of divinity. Anyone who is reborn in this way becomes a
hero, a semi-divine being."[4]

The principal element in baptism is water. As a symbol, water is
of great importance and universally refers to the most primal source
of life itself. In the biblical account, the waters are there in the beginning as the primal, undifferentiated matter, i.e., the Latin
materia. This idea is universal in myth; all life comes from the waters. Jung's studies have established the fact that water is the prime
symbol for the transpersonal unconscious. As noted earlier, Jung
used the term *personal unconscious* for the aspect of the psyche
that carries all the repressed material that could be conscious. The
transpersonal unconscious or the *collective unconscious* are terms
for the vast unknown depths of the psyche beyond the personal.
The words *collective* and *transpersonal* indicate the universality of
structure that Jung found in this aspect of the psyche. Just as the
human body has a universal anatomical structure whose details vary
infinitely, so Jung found that the psyche has a universal structure
whose details vary infinitely. The archetypes of the transpersonal
psyche are the universal structural features. The archetypes, however, do not appear directly to consciousness; instead, they are
manifested by symbols called archetypal images. The archetypal
images vary somewhat from one culture to another, but a family resemblance is usually quite detectable, and some images, like water,
are universal. Thus, wherever we turn in myth, water symbolizes
the source of all life, the foundation of the psyche, the matter out of
which come all things.

The connections between *materia* and *mater*, mother, are no
accident. Water, symbolically the mother, the maternal aspect of
water, as in baptism, coincides with the transpersonal psyche, for
the transpersonal psyche is always the mother of ego-consciousness. Water is thus symbolically not only the mother from whom
comes the phenomenal world but the mother from whom comes

ego-consciousness itself, i.e., knowing the world. "The waters, in short, symbolize the universal congress of potentialities, the *fons et origo*, which precedes all form and all creation." The symbolism of water is not only positive, however; it also is that to which life returns after it has run its course. "All living things rise, like the sun, from water, and sink into it again at evening. Born of springs, rivers, lakes, and seas, man at death comes to the waters of the Styx, and there embarks on the 'night sea journey.' Those black waters of death . . . with its cold embrace is the maternal womb, just as the sea devours the sun but brings it forth again."[5] Each transformation, including biological death, is a return to the waters, a rite of death and rebirth.

As the symbolism makes clear, rites of rebirth belong to matriarchal transformation mysteries, even when, as Neumann noted, the "symbolism or interpretation bears a patriarchal disguise." The water, as the symbol representing the very fountain and origin of life, refers not only to the original gift of life but to the spiritual principle that animates life and lures it forward in evolution in the spirit. "In the mysteries of rebirth the individual is . . . initiated by the spirit mother. . . . the Feminine as 'creative principle' encompasses the whole world. This is the totality of nature in its original unity, from which all life arises and unfolds, assuming, in its highest transformation, the form of spirit."[6]

Baptism, as recognized in the symbolism of most Christian groups who baptize by immersion, is a symbol of death in the waters and a rising from the waters to new life in the spirit. The transformation symbolism is obvious, but too often the meaning of the death in the waters is either unnoticed or trivialized because the connection with psychic transformation has been lost. The water in baptism is the symbol for the spiritual aspect of the feminine transformative character. What is to be transformed must enter wholly into the feminine principle; that is, it dies in returning to the Mother Vessel, the womb of the unconscious. Renewal is possible only through the death of the old personality.[7]

A second factor that has made it difficult for modern people to grasp the full meaning of the symbolism in baptism is the radical separation of spirit and matter that has occurred in the West. This dualism dates, of course, as far back as the Greeks, but in modern dress it was taught by John Locke in England and Descartes in France and became part of the basic myth of the West. That dualism was not presumed in traditional myth. A familiar mythic theme is the light that is found in darkness; for example, in the Bible, Jonah "sees the light" in the belly of the great sea monster. Jesus is described as the light that shone in the darkness, and the hymn in Isaiah, chapter 9, points out that "The people who walked in darkness have seen a great light." This idea of the healing power inherent in matter, in the body, so to speak, is also found in more modern therapeutic thought, in the generally recognized principle that the cure must come from within. The insight, the guidance, that is needed for healing is present in the person just as the conflict or the disease is present. More generally, we might say that this is the realization that the life principle, that which is the ultimate source of life wherever it appears, is part and parcel of everything.

Transformation is always preceded by a return flow of psychic energy, or in another figure, the shift of psychic dynamism, from ego-consciousness to the unconscious, back to the depths. Any such process is, of course, a dangerous one. If, instead of continuing on the journey, the libido gets stuck in the fascinations of the unconscious, then all is lost. "But if the libido manages to tear itself loose and force its way up again, something like a miracle happens: the journey to the underworld was a plunge into the fountain of youth, and the libido, apparently dead, wakes to renewed fruitfulness."[8]

The one who plunges to the depths goes to the prenatal realm of the "Eternal Feminine," the world of archetypal possibilities where slumbers the "divine child," the germ of wholeness. Here can be found the "treasure hard to attain," the pearl of great price. "It is these inherent possibilities of 'spiritual' or 'symbolic' life and of progress which form the ultimate, though unconscious, goal of regression."[9]

A final note concerning the gift or the discovery of the reconciling symbol: whenever there is an inner conflict, a division within the psyche, two forces are warring for control. These two forces represent life-potentials that seem contrary to each other, but both are vital to the psyche. For the life process to continue in any fruitful way, for the psyche to continue its intended path of development, these two antagonistic forces must be transcended in a higher synthesis. This reconciliation is made possible by the inclusion of the forces in a reconciling symbol that in effect reforms both by giving them a loftier perspective. Such a symbol cannot be invented, nor can it be found in the world—it must come as a gift. The gift comes as a revelation, an inspiration, mediated through forces that are beyond consciousness in the transpersonal realm.

Understanding the necessity of the reconciling symbol and its coming as a gift from the transpersonal is the psychological statement of the theological principle of salvation by grace alone and that through faith. Faith, in this context, is represented by the ego's trust in the gift and the giver, a willingness to take the reconciling symbol religiously (with ultimate seriousness) and act upon it. Salvation, transformation, psychic restoration—none of these are deeds that can be wrought by ego; they must be received as gifts and apprehended by faith. The Apostle Paul seems to imply that idea when he advises the Phillipians, "work out your own salvation with fear and trembling; for God is at work in you, both to will and to work for his good pleasure" (2:12). The work of God in you is transpersonal.

To understand the symbols surrounding Jesus' baptism, consider some of the background in Israel's history. Prophecy had ceased in Israel some four hundred years before the birth of Jesus. It was a time of darkness in many, many ways—spiritual, political, social. Many faithful Israelites hoped for the Messiah and looked for the promised forerunner, Elijah, whose reappearance would set the stage for the Messiah's appearance. Elijah is the herald of the new age. The Gospel of St. Mark makes it clear that John the Baptizer is the prophet Elijah returned to inaugurate the new age. A most distinctive personality, Elijah practiced an austere manner of life and preached an uncompromising message. His clothing was a garment of coarse camel hair, which was girt about his loins with a leather girdle. His territory was the wilderness. Thus, when Mark tells us that John the Baptizer "appeared in the wilderness, preaching a baptism of repentance for the forgiveness of sins" and that he "was clothed with camel's hair, and had a leather girdle around his waist, and ate locusts and wild honey," we are being given all the clues necessary to identify him as Elijah in his promised reappearance (Mark 1:4–6; cf. 2 Kings 1:8).

The life of Elijah the prophet is characterized also by his unremitting war with Ahab and Ahab's wife, Jezebel. "Ahab did more to provoke the LORD, the God of Israel, to anger than all the kings of Israel who were before him" (1 Kings 16:32). The infamous deeds of Ahab were as follows: (1) He had married Jezebel, a daughter of Ethbaal, who was king of the Zidonians and a former priest of Astarte (Jezebel was a devoted worshiper of Baal and a deadly enemy of the prophets of the Lord of Israel). (2) Ahab himself served Baal and built a temple for Baal in Samaria. (3) Ahab made an Asherah, i.e., a symbol for the goddess Asherah, a deity known as Mistress of the Gods (because she was the mother of seventy gods) and also as the Lady of the Sea.

Jezebel was an assertive, aggressive woman, grasping for power and control. She had issued an order to kill the prophets of the Lord, and Ahab did nothing to stop its execution. Ahab's character and his relationship with Jezebel are also shown by the incident of Naboth's vineyard, which Ahab longed to own. Ahab was still a servant of his instincts, so when Naboth refused to sell the vineyard, Ahab went to bed sulking and refused to eat, clearly showing the earmarks of the spoiled child trying to manipulate the mother. Jezebel cooperated with Ahab's dark side very well by response. She plotted and carried out Naboth's execution on false charges. Ahab gladly accepted the results, thus binding himself even more firmly to his instinctual demands and his Shadow side. By their characters, Ahab and Jezebel are fitting symbols for those whose ego-consciousness requires transformation, who have not transcended the instincts and faced their own Shadows.

Elijah, by contrast, confronts Ahab and Jezebel on behalf of the Lord and is thus a fitting symbol for the power of the psyche that calls the ego to mature, to take charge of instinctual forces through the process of transformation, to face the Shadow. But neither the king nor his wife are in the least looking for any word from the

Lord, any reconciling symbol; they are firmly in league with the renegade forces of the psyche.

John's baptism is also quite suited to his role as the returned Elijah, for it was a baptism of repentance. John's message was an uncompromising call to repent lest one evoke the wrath of God and to follow repentance with righteousness. He sternly warned those whose lives did not bear the fruit of righteousness that their claim that Abraham was their father would not save them on the day of judgment. Charity to the poor and scrupulous honesty were demanded. Hence, John is also a fitting figure to represent the forces of the psyche that demand that ego grow beyond its subservience to the instinctual drives in order to take responsibility for the acts of the person. John thus stands against the forces of the instinctual aspect of the psyche, which in myth is represented by the dark side of the Great Mother Goddess and by the various goddess figures (e.g., Asherah) who incarnate her image.

The early Christians were scandalized by the story of Jesus' baptism at John's hands because they had come to think of Jesus as having no dark side, in the terms of analytical psychology, no Shadow. In fact, the early church had from its origin found it difficult to affirm Jesus' humanity as anything more than abstract theory. The dualistic thinking of late Judaism and of Babylon and Persia was prominent among Christians too, despite Jesus' own holistic thought. This dualism split the universe and all its parts into good versus evil, light versus dark. They could not imagine Jesus as anything but pure light, pure good; hence, his being baptized into repentance for the forgiveness of sins made no sense to them.

The Gospel texts also make it clear that Jesus' ministry was on a higher plane than John's. "I have baptized you with water; but he will baptize you with the Holy Spirit" (Mark 1:8). Jesus does call people to a higher level of psychic development than John does. John is not an innovator, not a Hero figure of mythic dimension. Even John questioned Jesus' need for repentance and baptism: "I need to be baptized by you, and do you come to me?" To which Jesus responds, "Let it be so now; for thus it is fitting for us to fulfil all righteousness" (Matt. 3:14–15). The Hero is not born fully developed psychically any more than he is fully developed physically. He, too, must know and overcome his own instinctual drives. "Therefore he had to be made like his brethren in every respect" (Heb. 2:17).

The first foundation of civilization is the development of ego-consciousness to a level that is sufficient to control the instinctual drives. The basic instincts are for food, sex, and power, especially power over one's environment. Freud's psychology is built on the assumption that all psychic energy is sexual. Alfred Adler assumed that the central psychic energy is the drive for power by and for the ego. Jung, recognizing the partial truth in both assumptions, incorporates and transcends both Freud and Adler. All agree that a necessary part of psychic development is to gain control over these instincts. Biblically, the Canaanites, in their Baal worship, symbolize an almost unrestrained capitulation to instinct. Egypt, earlier in Israelite history, played the same role symbolically. To the Israelites, who had the sternness of Mosaic Law in addition to priestly enforcement to help keep them straight, the Canaanites seemed morally inferior, degenerate, lustful, and unprincipled. Even the name suggests the problem: Canaan, the youngest son of Noah, is described as a shameless and perverse man, which is a good description of one who still lives mostly at the instinctual level. The Canaanites were still practicing Mother-right religion, worshiping the goddesses, and as they were considered morally inferior, the Israelites concluded that the Canaanite religion was of no value, or even decidedly evil. These considerations also supported the patriarchal, solar religion of Israel and their sense of exclusiveness as the chosen people. Jesus' baptism at the hands of John is thus symbolically his call to stand against the instinctual forces by daring to plunge into their depths and overcome them.

The Hero must conquer his infantile tie to the Mother by gaining access to her symbolic equivalent. In the tie to the Mother unconscious lie the Hero's extraordinary powers, which are freed by the battle with the paralyzing forces of the unconscious. The unconscious is the source of all creativity, "but it needs heroic courage to do battle with these forces and to wrest from them the treasure hard to attain."[10] In the Hero myth, ego and consciousness become the bearers of psychic development against the negative powers of the unconscious. This state is played out symbolically in initiation rites in which young men are removed from the maternal world and reborn as children of the spirit, sons of heaven, not just sons of earth. The male group requires the individual to act as an independent, responsible person; thus, initiation always involves the testing and the strengthening of consciousness. The classic Hero is one who has been granted a spiritual vision and a direct relationship with the Ultimate Spirit. For the community that the Hero founds, the founder and the Ultimate Spirit are one. Moses, after his vision at Sinai, acquires the features of Yahweh and must be veiled. From this comes the sacred formula "I and the Father are One."

> And when he came up out of the water, immediately he saw the heavens opened and the Spirit descending upon him like a dove; and a voice came from heaven, "Thou art my beloved Son; with thee I am well pleased."
> The Spirit immediately drove him out into the wilderness. And he was in the wilderness forty days, tempted by Satan; and he was with the wild beasts; and the angels ministered to him. (Mark 1:10–13)

The Hero has a dual nature, i.e., a divinely begotten nature as well as the usual human nature. The basis for this duality is not only the community, to whom he must appear as divine simply because he transcends their human norm, but his own inner experience. "He discovers within himself something which, although it 'belongs' to him and is as it were part of him, he can only describe as strange, unusual, godlike." Because he does transcend the norm of the humanity about him and because he experiences this greater power within, he feels inspired, the son of a god. "Heavenly succor, the feeling of being rooted up aloft in the father divinity, who is not just head of the family but a creative spirit, alone makes possible the fight with the dragon of the Great Mother."[11]

For a man the departure and initiation can also be looked upon psychologically as the constellation of the anima within the psyche. Jung used *anima* to describe the soul of a man, *animus* the soul of a woman. For Jung, soul meant the inner personality with which one

faces the unconscious. He also spoke of this figure as a mediator between ego and the collective unconscious, especially that central
figure of the whole psyche, the Self, the God image that dominates
or is the central principle of the psyche. Neumann relates the
anima to the "transformative character" of the feminine principle of
the psyche. "It is the mover, the instigator of change, whose fascination drives, lures, and encourages the male to all the adventures
of the soul and spirit, of action and creation in the inner and the
outward world."[12] The "elementary character" of the feminine
tends to dissolve the ego and consciousness in the unconscious;
hence, it is the dragon aspect, the instincts that must be overcome.
By contrast, the "transformative character," for which the anima is
the vehicle par excellence, sets the personality in motion, leading
to change and ultimately to transformation.

Neither Jung nor Neumann, nor any other of the analytical psychologists, has worked out fully or satisfactorily the comparable
process of development for the feminine Heroine journey. There
are few stories of Heroines, probably because the myths that have
come down through history to us have been transmitted through
three or more millennia of patriarchal cultures. The Greek story of
Psyche is one possible example; another is the biblical account of
Ruth. Certainly each of these women overcame the dragon of the
unconscious instincts and went on to overcome the second
dragon—culture. The general pattern of the Hero's journey seems
common to both men and women, though there are clearly variations within it. I cannot, within the scope of this book, develop an
independent account of the Heroine, but I hope that the story of
the Hero will shed considerable light on the story of the Heroine,
for whom the contrasexual guide would be the animus figure.

In the battle with the instincts, the battle to overcome finally
the possessive character of the Great Mother, the anima confronts
the Ego-Hero with a "trial," a testing that he must undergo successfully to pass on to the next stage of psychic development.
Victory at this point means not only a more powerful ego-consciousness and a more responsible ego-consciousness but a reorganization of the forces in the collective unconscious in the
interest of transformation. This reorganization is the beginning of

the integration of the psyche, the wedding of the masculine and feminine aspects.

The Greek myth of Phaeton illustrates well the perils or the testing that the Hero must undergo at this point. In this story Phaeton, born of a virgin, taunted by playmates about his missing father, goes in search of the father. His mother has told him that his father is Phoebus, the god who drives the solar chariot. Phaeton sets off across Persia and India in search of his father's palace, at last finds it, and there meets his father, who gathers Phaeton into his arms and claims him as son, promising him whatever he desires. Phaeton asks for the right to drive his father's chariot with the winged horses. That request represents a clear case of inflation. The ego has taken the identification with the father literally and is claiming the prerogatives of God. This is the pride that goeth before a fall. Phaeton represents the ego, which will use its newly discovered identity for ego-glorification. Phaeton, of course, demands that his father fulfill the promise and drives the winged horse chariot to his own doom, falling to earth in flames, like a falling star.

The initiation of the Hero is the crossing of a threshold from the world of the mothers to the world of the fathers. The crossing symbolizes the attaining of independence, leaving behind childhood dependence, the realm of the mothers. The initiating priest is to entrust power only to one who has demonstrated that he will not fall prey to inflation. The symbols of office will finally be given only to one who has been purged of infantile selfishness, of the need for ego-glorification, of personal preference or resentment. The Hero must demonstrate that he is twice born, that he truly represents the love of God, which bathes the universe like an impersonal cosmic force that sends sun and rain on the just and the unjust alike.

So we read in Mark 1:13 that Jesus, having been driven into the wilderness by the Spirit, was there forty days, tempted by Satan, and he was with the wild beasts, and the angels ministered to him. We may connect the spirit here with the anima, the spirit who will lead the Hero beyond the realm of phenomenality, beyond the realm of attachment to the ego. The anima relates the ego to the deeper layers of the psyche and clarifies values; helps the Hero discover his proper identity and destiny as the true child of the father; and protects as well as guides through the ego-shattering initiation by the father.

The Satan figure of the Bible may be connected with the Shadow, the dark, unknown side of the personality that "normally encounters the ego, the centre and representative of the light side and of consciousness, in the form of a dark, uncanny figure of evil— to confront whom is always a fateful experience for the individual."[13] At first, one experiences the figure of the Shadow in projected externalized form, as an alien enemy. As the elements of the personal Shadow are gradually incorporated into consciousness through identification, acceptance of ownership, and assimilation, a deeper factor—the archetypal Shadow—remains potent in the depths of the psyche. It is the archetypal Shadow that is appropriately called the devil or adversary, the tempter figure. Mythic material often depicts the Shadow as the dark brother of the Hero, as in the pairs Osiris and Set, Abel and Cain, Jacob and Esau, Faust and Mephisto. Dr. Jekyll and Mr. Hyde likewise are representations of this dual figure, the Hero-Shadow. In short the Satan or Shadow figure represents the inherent evil in humanity, our original sin, our God-opposing will.

In "A Psychological Approach to the Trinity" Jung identifies Lucifer as the personification of the God-opposing will:

> But for this will there would have been no creation and no work of salvation either. The shadow and the opposing will are the necessary conditions for all actualization. An object that has no will of its own, capable, if need be, of opposing its creator, and with no qualities other than its creator's, such an object has no independent existence and is incapable of ethical decision. . . . Therefore Lucifer was perhaps the one who best understood the divine will struggling to create a world and who carried out that will most faithfully. For, by rebelling against God, he became the active principle of a creation which opposed to God a counter-will of its own.[14]

In his discussion of the Shadow Neumann writes as follows:

> In every case, the acceptance of the shadow is preceded by a mortal conflict, in which the ego struggles to the last to defend its own world of values; it is only through suffering that it finally arrives at an awareness

of a new ethic, in which the ego and the conscious mind are no longer responsible for the sole and ultimate decision. At first, for both patient and therapist, the shadow is Evil—and Evil is that which is to be avoided. . . . The change of attitude towards the shadow which is essential for the healing of the sick person, who is the representative of modern man in all his splitness and disintegration, has nothing in common with any megalomaniac condition of being "beyond good and evil." On the contrary, the acceptance of oneself as including a dark aspect and a shadow actually springs from a deep and humble recognition of the invincible creatureliness of man, which is a part of the purpose of his creation.[15]

"The Shadow is the 'guardian of the threshold,' across which the path leads into the nether realm of transformation and renewal. And so what first appears to the ego as a devil becomes a psychopomp, a guide of the soul, who leads the way into the underworld of the unconscious."[16] This is the realm of healing and of creativity. From this deep realm the healing and restorative energies pour forth into the world through the Hero.

We may thus conclude that in the story of Jesus, the spirit-anima drives him to confront his Shadow, personified and projected as Satan, the inner tempter. The first and the second temptations begin with the words "If you are the Son of God." These words suggest immediately that Jesus' temptation is to inflation, as was Phaeton's. The specific form is cast by these words: "command these stones to become loaves of bread" (Matt. 4:3) or "command this stone to become bread" (Luke 4:3). If we treat this as a mythic statement or a dream fragment, we look for associations with stone and bread. The obvious first thought is to take them at face value, and indeed, much sense is made that way. The temptation would then represent Jesus using his power as magic: he would be dreaming the dream of modern technology; he would save the world by solving its material problems. Jesus is depicted in both these accounts as having fasted for forty days, during which he was tempted but following which "he was hungry." The Gospel writers record the first temptation as having occurred at that point. Doubtless they presumed that Jesus had thought much about the hungry of the world, had felt much compassion for the downtrodden, and that he would have been tempted to use his powers to help them. This

idea alone, however, makes his answer seem a bit weak: "It is written, 'Man shall not live by bread alone, but by every word that proceeds from the mouth of God.' "

Stone is an important word in the New Testament, and using
the principle of amplification as we would with a dream, we are jus-
tified in looking beyond the obvious. *Stone* suggests Jesus as cor-
nerstone, Peter as the stone on which the Church is to be founded,
a stone of stumbling for Jesus. In these connections, *stone* seems to
mean the Christ principle, i.e., the spiritual identity of Jesus as the
Christ, the Son of God, the Hero. What would it mean for the
Hero to turn his identity into bread? It could mean to devote his
power to earthly affairs and goals, seeking to build up his ego by his
great deeds for the world. He would then be regarded as a great
world hero. Or he could claim the glory of the Son of God for the
ego by becoming a great spiritual leader, commanding loyalty to
God. In either possibility the Shadow is urging a way of thought
contrary to the way of growth for the psyche. All three of the temptations concern the proper relationship of the ego to the new identity proclaimed at baptism.

Jesus answered the first temptation by quoting from Deuteronomy a passage which explains what the Israelites were to have
learned from their experience of forty years in the wilderness.
Forty years, like *forty days*, is a mythological or symbolic term,
meaning essentially the right length of time. Four is a divine
number, the symbol of completion or wholeness, and so is forty.
This passage makes clear the teaching-learning intent of the wilderness: God was

> "testing you to know what was in your heart, whether you would keep
> his commandments, or not. And he humbled you and let you hunger
> . . . that he might make you know that man does not live by bread
> alone, but that man lives by everything that proceeds out of the mouth
> of the LORD." (Deut. 8:2–3)

Psychologically, in the economy of the psyche, the message is that
the ego must not prefer its own material welfare or its own glory to
the necessity of the spiritual quest, the attending and following of
the inner voice.

The second temptation begins with the same formula, "If you are the Son of God," but in a different context. Satan has transported Jesus to the pinnacle of the temple in Jerusalem, the holy city. The holy city is the dwelling place of God; the temple in particular is his habitation. Psychologically, the temple means the center of the psyche, the Self. The temptation is cast in these words, "If you are the Son of God, throw yourself down; for it is written, 'He will give his angels charge of you,' and 'On their hands they will bear you up, lest you strike your foot against a stone'" (Matt. 4:6). Jesus again quotes Deuteronomy, this time from 6:16, "You shall not put the LORD your God to the test," to which is added in the original, "as you tested him at Massah."

The event at Massah, recorded in two places in Scripture, does not clearly describe the sin of Moses. The people, according to the account, were suffering from a shortage of water and contended with Moses and Aaron. "Why have you brought the assembly of the LORD into this wilderness, that we should die here, both we and our cattle?" (Num. 20:4). This grumbling and lack of faith are typical of the temper that Moses' Israelite followers displayed whenever they got into a tight spot. The odd part of the story is the punishment of Aaron and Moses, who, according to the account, manifest no particular lack of faith, nor does the account mention any act of arrogance.

The Lord says to Moses and Aaron, when they bring the people's complaint before him,

> "Take the rod, and assemble the congregation, you and Aaron your brother, and tell the rock before their eyes to yield its water; so you shall bring water out of the rock for them; so you shall give drink to the congregation and their cattle." (Num. 20:8)

But no sooner have they carried out the order than the following message comes from on high, "And the Lord said to Moses and Aaron, 'Because you did not believe in me, to sanctify me in the eyes of the people of Israel, therefore you shall not bring this assembly into the land which I have given them'" (Num. 20:12). To that message is added a specific death sentence for Aaron "because you rebelled against my command at the waters of Meribah" (Num.

20:24). A possible clue to the sin of Moses and Aaron is in Numbers 20:10: Moses says to the assembly gathered before the rock, "Hear now, you rebels; shall we bring forth water for you out of this rock?" Were the Lord's servants claiming divine authority so as to "put the Lord to the test"? Whatever our answer may be to this puzzle, it seems that later generations made this event the source of the aphorism "You shall not tempt the Lord."

Psychologically, the ego that has begun to experience its identification with the Self is often caught up in inflation because the ego is identifying with its transcendent source and claiming that power or right as its own. This power claim may be acted out in the world as a form of megalomania or as simple arrogance. All the temptations are to interpret the new spiritual identity as belonging to the ego, to one's surface identity. In the testing of Jesus as exemplary Hero, this temptation seems to mean a desire to force God to prove by some publicly visible evidence that the inner experience of sonship is true, that the inflated sense of identity is factual, and that ego thus deserves acclaim from others. The arrogance of the fresh convert to any religion or ism is manifestation of this pattern. Such wallowing in inflation is the end of psychological or spiritual development and thus must be proscribed. "The meaning of all these processes lies in strengthening the principle of Ego consciousness. But the danger inherent in this line of development is exaggerated self-importance, a megalomaniac Ego consciousness which thinks itself independent of everything."[17]

In the last temptation, as recorded in Matthew, the devil takes Jesus to a very high mountain from which the devil shows him all the kingdoms of the world and the glory of them; and the devil says, "All these I will give you, if you will fall down and worship me" (Matt. 4:9). A Faustian note sounds in this temptation. The legend of Faust seems to be built on the historical foundation of Dr. Johannes Faust of Swabis, of the sixteenth century, who traveled widely, performed magical feats, and died under mysterious circumstances. According to the legend he sold his soul to the devil in exchange for youth, knowledge, and magical power. Many stories have been woven out of the legend. In 1593 Christopher Marlowe wrote the play *The Tragical History of Dr. Faustus*, in which the doctor, through his pact with the devil, seeks to gain physical and intellectual satisfaction but fails because his moral pride is too great for him to admit and recant his sins (i.e., to face his own Shadow). Lessing saw in Faust the personification of man's heroic striving for knowledge and power. Goethe elevated him to a more philosophical seeker.

Perhaps the third temptation can be equated with the human temptation to put ultimate trust in rational, pragmatic human reason, in the form of political realism, for example. Time and again in the modern world we have seen this trust lead to the hope that government can bring about some utopian state. It easily leads to the form of ego-inflation that dreams of great power, of being a universal ruler of world peace and unity. In the Old Testament we see this vain hope as the destruction both of David and of Solomon. It is the classic temptation for all politicians and many others. Even some recent American presidents seem to have been infected with the dream of being leaders of world peace and unity, and in a particularly virulent form, it nearly destroyed Europe under Hitler and the Nazi madness.

Again Jesus responds from the tradition, "You shall worship the Lord your God and him only shall you serve." God is not to be subordinated to any other, not to ego-temptation to power, not even to make the world better. Every scheme to improve the lot of mankind by human reason and its tools seems to end up glorifying the schemer but to leave the poor much as it found them. The true Hero must have all such ambitions and ego-trips well identified and put behind him before he is ready to be trusted with the supreme power of the Son of God. In the Hero there is to be no place whatever for ego-aggrandizement.

It is the normal pattern of development that the ego will overreach itself. Only when the ego is properly chastened, humbled, and enlightened by its growth toward the Self does another possibility emerge. In the temptation story, after Jesus denies the lure of ego inflation (the wiles of the satanic tempter), "Then the devil left him, and behold, angels came and ministered to him" (Matt. 4:11). When the ego becomes aware of its own limits and dependence on the transpersonal psyche, it becomes the recipient of new and mysterious support—the angels of God appear. Jesus had now not only identity and commitment but an inner sense of peace, wholeness, and support. The change showed in his demeanor; the people who had known him were astonished at the change. "Where did this man get this wisdom? Is not this the carpenter's son?" (Matt. 13:54; cf. Luke 4:22).

The Gospel of Luke adds to this story a note that makes it more applicable to all of us and strengthens the human picture of Jesus: the tempter left Jesus to await a more opportune time. Few will emerge from a single wilderness experience not only unscathed but empowered. The wilderness itself can be a crushing experience in which we come face-to-face with the dark possibilities that are our very own. Satan is not just an external figure who lures us the wrong way but the very essence of evil in our own lives, in our souls. It is, furthermore, a considerable comedown for the inflated ego to realize that the power of the transpersonal Self does not and cannot belong to the ego or be controlled by it; the ego is to be servant, not master, even in its own psychic domain. The wilderness experience is necessary to bring down the inflation of the ego, which cannot expect or receive the support of the Self until it has been freed from its inflated identification with the Self. As Luther described it, "God works by contraries so that a man feels himself to be lost in the very moment when he is on the point of being saved."[18]

VIII

The Battle
with the Dragon

HAVING PASSED SUCCESSFULLY through the wilderness
of temptation, the Hero has brought the uncontrolled instinctual
side of himself under control, has become the equal of the inner
tempter, has met the Shadow and accepted it as part of his being
but without having been either crushed or repelled. This battle is a
milestone in the process of spiritual development.

Jesus' victory was a most important one for his historical situation. A few moments' reflection on life under Roman rule will help
to put things in perspective. That ancient world was one of incredible brutality; thoughtless, mindless instinct ruled the day. As Jung
noted, Christianity was accepted in the early Roman world "as a
means of escape from the brutality and unconsciousness of the ancient world."[1] To the everlasting credit of Christianity it offered a
way of bringing the instincts under control, of escaping the mindless world of instinctual rule. Jewish law had already begun this
process, but the law, until it has been subjected to the critique of
an awakened consciousness, is an external force of control, not an
internal one; although the law offers control, it is control through
willed, often fearful, obedience, not the response of the heart.

Jesus the cultural Hero shows that the way forward in spiritual
development is the path of personal power over the instinctual
forces and that following the path means allying the ego with the
power of the transpersonal Self, recognizing oneself as a "child of
God," i.e., a "Son of God." This message is as important today as it
was then, for our primitive, instinctual personalities are covered by

only a thin layer of civilization, a layer that is held in place only by tenuous religious conviction. When that conviction disappears, the old mass brutalization quickly returns, as the events of Nazi Germany and Stalinist Russia should teach us readily enough.

It is doubtful whether any morality of note is possible without the kind of religious insight into human life offered by Christianity (and other world religions). As Jean Paul Sartre observed, if there is no God, all things are permitted. The contemporary world political and economic situation seems to attest that uncontrolled greed and self-interest do not form a very solid political or economic foundation. "We like to imagine that our primitive traits have long since disappeared without trace. In this we are cruelly disappointed, for never before has our civilization been so swamped with evil. This gruesome spectacle helps us to understand what Christianity was up against and what it endeavoured to transform."[2]

The overcoming of instinctual forces from the depths of our psyche is not by any means the end of the battle for spiritual development. This first skirmish is a critical one, but it only results in overcoming, at least in part, the gross sins of the flesh. Beyond lie the sins of the spirit—avarice, pride, and envy. In myth this higher level of conflict is often symbolized by the dragon tyrant, Holdfast, who is firmly ensconced in the seat of social power, which he uses for his own benefit. "The inflated ego of the tyrant is a curse to himself and his world—no matter how his affairs may seem to prosper. Self-terrorized, fear-haunted, alert at every hand to meet and battle back the anticipated aggressions of his environment, which are primarily the reflections of the uncontrollable impulses to acquisition within himself, the giant of self-achieved independence is the world's messenger of disaster, even though in his mind, he may entertain himself with humane intentions."[3]

Remember that the material under consideration is the New Testament mythology, not scholarly history. This symbolic approach does not depend only upon the historians' findings concerning the probable facts of the various New Testament figures. The New Testament uses the figures in a symbolic way that often disagrees with current scholarly history. I am trying to reveal the symbolic meaning. Projection often colors experience and clouds perspective. It is obvious that the early church, in whose environs the New Testament came to birth, was not neutral about Judaism or about the Jewish leaders of that day. The factual basis for the negative feelings was the persecution that at least some of them experienced. But equally important for our note here is the psychological phenomenon by which the stage from which we have just emerged in our growth is typically undervalued, even scapegoated, its faults remembered and exaggerated and its virtues ignored or forgotten. Thus, after the Reformation, the Protestants remembered and regarded the Roman Catholic Church as their enemy, a corrupt, dangerous, ungodly institution, whose leader was the anti-Christ. In addition, in this new and always tenuous state, we invariably project our repressed negative characteristics onto the perceived enemy, often a minority group. For Americans the classic target has been those groups not of WASP background, particularly blacks. A foreign group perceived as enemy is typically perceived as much by projections as by reality; for example, the Russians are credited with many of the worst features of Americans, whether deserved or not, and vice versa. To grasp the intensity of this problem, contrast the communist picture of the bloated, selfish, and ruthless capitalist and the reality of most American business leaders.

Thus, when the Hero journey reaches the stage at which independence of thought and action is necessary, it is the perceived tyrant father (culture) who becomes the archetypal symbol. In the following discussion I will follow more or less the conventional view of Israel's history, as set forth by Noth (even though newer studies are questioning the accuracy of those views) and will simply accept the New Testament view of its Israelite past without questioning historical accuracy. My concern here is archetypal symbolism, not history. For example, Nehemiah and Ezra are treated in the Old Testament as contemporaries, but in history, they probably were not.

In Israel there was no single tyrant (unless he might be symbolized by the chief priest) but rather a tyrant institution—primitive Judaism—the leaders of which formed the collective tyranny that Jesus was to oppose. Judaism was founded, after the exile a century or so earlier, under the leadership of Nehemiah and Ezra, whose

followers included the second generation of the returnees from captivity. (Much of the history is unknown or debatable, and the biblical records freely mix the mythic and the historic.) Nehemiah's
goal, along with that of Ezra the priest, was the restoration of Jerusalem. Nehemiah and Ezra, who can only be described as "ethnic
purists" and strict isolationists, became the natural leaders of the
returning deportees from Babylon (who, by and large, held very
strict views) and advocated the rigorous observance of the law of
Moses as the foundation for the whole of life.

Nehemiah concerned himself mainly with the rebuilding of the
city and the temple and with the governing of the city. Ezra's work
was to be the enforcement of the sacred law. Nehemiah was author-
ized in his endeavor by the Persian ruler, and with this power, sub-
mission to this law became the decisive token of membership in
Israel and the religious community in Jerusalem. The earlier organic unity of Israel (i.e., unity of common history and common liberation after exile, not amphictyony, as Noth thought) was now
replaced by the group who acknowledged the law. As Noth comments, "It is obvious that the meaning which the divine law
thereby acquired for Israel was bound to become extraordinarily
important, not only for its outward but also for its spiritual life."[4]
The law came to be regarded increasingly as a revelation of the divine king, obedience to whom was to be total and without question.
Worship, too, was transformed, losing something of its spontaneous
"rejoicing before the Lord" and more and more becoming devoted
to the scrupulous fulfillment of the "law of the God of Heaven."
This devotion to law easily expanded to the sanctification of the
books containing the law, hence the formation of the Holy Book,
which was binding on the whole of the religious community. (The
law at this point probably existed and functioned more in the realm
of what psychoanalytic thought calls primary process thinking, in
which there is little differentiation between image and reality; by
the New Testament period, law is in the secondary process of more
objective consciousness.)

Nehemiah and Ezra were Heroes of the restoration of Israel.
Before them, Moses was the Hero-founder of Israel. Each represented the Father God to the community. But as time passes, a de-

terioration may set in, either in the character of the Hero or in the community established by the Hero. The Zoroastrian legend of the Emperor of the Golden Age, Jemshid, exemplifies such a crisis:

> All looked upon the throne, and heard and saw
> Nothing but Jemshid, he alone was King,
> Absorbing every thought; and in their praise
> And adoration of that mortal man,
> Forgot the worship of the great Creator.[5]

The community thus established may seem to be, or promise to be, a paradise in comparison with the dependency of mother-rule, but it is, like an adolescent gang, for us and ours only. The paradise includes a "hate-the-common-enemy" philosophy. It was in criticism of this philosophy that Jesus said, "You have heard that it was said, 'You shall love your neighbor and hate your enemy.' But I say to you, Love your enemies and pray for those who persecute you, so that you may be sons of your Father who is in heaven; for he makes his sun rise on the evil and on the good, and sends rain on the just and on the unjust" (Matt. 5:43–45).

An ethnocentric community is necessarily caught in a projection of its own Shadow onto the despised enemy. The enemy then can and will be publicly hated and derided as totally bad, an agent of the Evil One, always to be distrusted for the very faults that belong to the Shadow of the ethnocentric group. Ego is not curbed in exclusive groups; instead, its self-righteous and self-aggrandizing tendencies are increased. Modern examples of this self- and culture-destroying pattern are the projection of the Nazi Shadow onto the Jews and the mutual projection of a lust to control the world by the United States and Russia, thus ensuring a continual blind distrust and murderous hatred of each other.[6]

By the time of Jesus' life, obedience to a tangible law had more apparent reality and social binding power than did worship of and obedience to a Creator God, who had come to seem remote. The nearness of the law versus the apparent remoteness of God is a state of great tragedy, for it represents the loss of any direct relationship with God, with the creative source. Consequently, the culture decayed, and the great cry for a savior was heard through-

out the land. " 'Legitimate' faith must always rest on experience,"
writes Jung. But there is another kind of "faith," a secondhand
faith, based on the authority of tradition, i.e., someone else's experience, which is hypothesized as authoritative and binding. Under
this aegis, the traditional contents gradually lose their meaning,
and the faith based on them has no living power behind it. When
the experience behind the faith is lost, "faith is only another word
for habitual, infantile dependence, which takes the place of, and actually prevents, the struggle for deeper understanding."[7] The tragic
dimensions of this plight cannot be overstated. When the basic
mythic faith of a culture loses its power, when the collective faith-
experience of the culture is weak or lost, all things begin to grind to
a stop. The culture starts to disintegrate and misery to abound, and
the cry for a savior goes up to heaven.

We are now in a better position to understand Jung's comment
that the Hero must do battle with both parents. The mother represents the inertia and instinctuality of the unconscious, and the father, the imprisonment of a sterile collective or an institution; both
block the way to further spiritual development. At the same time it
is from the unconscious that the creativity and power must come to
conquer the dragons.

After the forty days of temptation Jesus "returned in the power
of the Spirit into Galilee." He is remarkably different after the wilderness experiences. The ministering angels and the empowering
Spirit have done their work well. "The crowds were astonished at
his teaching, for he taught them as one who had authority, and not
as their scribes" (Matt. 7:28–29). His new power is such that

> a report concerning him went out through all the surrounding country.
> And he taught in their synagogues, being glorified by all. (Luke 4:14–
> 15). . . so that they were astonished and said, "Where did this man get
> this wisdom and these mighty works? Is not this the carpenter's
> son?". . . And they took offense at him. (Matt. 13:54–55, 57)

The fourth chapter of Luke tells us a bit more about the reason
for the offense taken at Jesus. Luke portrays Jesus in the synagogue
at Nazareth; there, on the sabbath, in a customary act, he stood up
to read:

And there was given to him the book of the prophet Isaiah. He opened
the book and found the place where it was written,
"The Spirit of the Lord is upon me,
because he has anointed me to preach good news to the poor.
He has sent me to proclaim release to the captives
and recovering of sight to the blind,
to set at liberty those who are oppressed,
to proclaim the acceptable year of the Lord." (Luke 4:17–19)

Thus far, no offense, but now Jesus sat down and began to bait the
Father dragon in his den:

"Today this scripture has been fulfilled in your hearing. . . . Doubtless
you will quote to me this proverb, 'Physician, heal yourself; what we
have heard you did at Capernaum, do here also in your own country.' "
. . . "Truly, I say to you, no prophet is acceptable in his own country."
(Luke 4:21, 23–24)

Mark adds to our knowledge by noting that the people in Nazareth
were so unresponsive to Jesus that he could do no mighty work
there, indeed, that Jesus "marveled because of their unbelief."

The people of Nazareth wanted what Jesus had done in Capernaum, i.e., miracles of healing. But let us look at the healing reports from Capernaum. Apparently Jesus did heal a number of people of diseases and infirmities there, but more important is his activity in the synagogue at Capernaum. As Mark reports it, Jesus went into the synagogue and taught with authority, "And immediately there was in their synagogue a man with an unclean spirit" (Mark 1:23).

From whence he came, we do not know. Who he might have been
is not hinted. Even the fact that he was there at all is highly puzzling,
since those who were unclean were banished from corporate worship
and the community until such time as the necessary sin offering and
atonement ceremony had been accomplished in their behalf. Mark
only says that he appeared *immediately* after Jesus began to teach with
authority and not as the scribes. Even the content of Jesus' teaching is
withheld. Attention is concentrated, instead on the fact that whatever it
concerned, it prompted the revelation of the presence of an unclean
spirit in the synagogue. . . .
Old Testament law states that uncleanness disqualified one for divine worship and sacrifice, and religious offices could not be performed

> in an unclean place, *i.e.*, outside of Palestine. . . . The one thing about
> uncleanness that is of paramount importance in a discussion of Mark's
> Gospel is that a state of uncleanness resulting from any cause made one
> unable to worship God and signified a condition of sin in the individ-
> ual, a blemished relationship between one and God.[8]

This story invites comparison with an event of Old Testament
history in which a group of dissenters, under the leadership of
Korah the Levite, assembled to protest against Moses and Aaron on
the grounds that they had exalted themselves above the people of
Israel in their claims of leadership. The Old Testament episode,
found in Numbers, chapter 16, effectively depicts Korah as filled
with an unclean spirit; the result of their protest was that "the
ground under them split asunder; and the earth opened its mouth
and swallowed them up"(vs. 31–32).

> When Jesus was confronted by the unclean spirit in the place of
> congregation, that is, the synagogue, he rebuked it, saying. "Be silent,
> and come out of him!" (Mark 1:25) All who were gathered there were
> amazed and exclaimed: "What is this? A *new teaching*! With authority
> he commands even the unclean spirits, and they obey him." (v. 27,
> italics ours) As the unclean spirit embodied in the company of Korah
> and his followers was removed from the midst of the congregation by a
> *new* thing done by the Lord, and the people were left in no doubt as to
> whom God had chosen as the "holy one" to lead the people, so the un-
> clean spirit vanished from the congregation surrounding Jesus before a
> *new* teaching.[9]

The parallels in these stories lead to the inference that Mark is
drawing a comparison between the contests. In Mark the contest is
between Jesus, God's chosen leader, and the Levitical priesthood,
the spiritual guardians of the religious life of Israel. In Numbers it
was the Levites versus Moses and Aaron. An implied parallel exists
in the way Aaron was revealed to be God's "holy one" and the way
Jesus is revealed by his power over an unclean spirit. The lines of
the dragon battle have been drawn. As the Gospel of Mark develops, this conflict intensifies, for the Hero is battling more than a
single demon. There is a profound sickness in Israel itself; she is
the princess held in captivity "until the Son of God appear" to deliver her from the dragon forces symbolized by the Levitical priest-

hood. The dragon forces that the Hero now faces are those of the Terrible Father, and they must be overcome before the princess can be freed.

Who or what are the Terrible Fathers whom the Hero must overcome? Keeping in mind the pattern of patriarchal development under Ezra and Nehemiah, we need only to connect that pattern with mythic patterns in general. The fathers, as Neumann notes, are the representatives of law and order, from the earliest semblances to the modern judicial systems. "They hand down the highest values of civilization, whereas the mothers control the highest, *i.e.*, deepest, values of life and nature. The world of the fathers is thus the world of collective values."[10]

The fathers see to it that the coming generation is thoroughly invested with the collective values and devise ways of eliminating from the culture those who stray too far from the collective norm. The authoritative advocacy of the canon of values forms in the individual the directive voice known as conscience, or, as Freud named it, superego. The canon of values, elevated to the place of an absolute authority, must be opposed by the Hero. He must oppose it because the Hero's task is "to awaken the sleeping images of the future which can and must come forth from the night, in order to give the world a new and better face."[11]

Almost automatically the Hero is a breaker of the law, the enemy of the old ruling system and its leaders, a cultural rebel. In this conflict the "inner voice," the command of the transpersonal Father God, who wants the world to change, conflicts with the commands of the personal fathers who speak for the old law. We may draw a parallel here between Jesus and Abraham. The latter is told, "Go from your country and your kindred and your father's house to the land that I will show you" (Gen. 12:1). A midrash interprets this to mean that Abraham is to destroy the gods of his father. Just so, Jesus, who teaches with "authority and not as the scribes," literally violates the laws of the fathers and invites others to do the same.

Basically, the conflict in this battle is between two gods or two sets of god images, two different understandings of the will of God

for humankind, two myths. The Hero, as bringer of the new, is the
new manifestation of the Father Creator God. Mythologically, it is
wicked king (i.e., the patriarchal system) who sets the battles
through which the Hero demonstrates his heroism at this point in
spiritual development. The obstacles put in his way by the tyranny
of the patriarchs are the incentives to heroism. As Rank observed,
the mythic Hero in general, "by solving the tasks which the father
imposed with intent to destroy him, develops from a dissatisfied
son to a socially valuable reformer, a conqueror of man-eating mon-
sters that ravage the countryside, an inventor, a founder of cities
and bringer of culture."[12]

Fundamentally, the battle of the Hero is always for the continued development of consciousness and responsibility and against
unconsciousness and dependence. So long as the battle is against
the forces of unconsciousness, the Hero is in conflict with the Great
and Terrible Mother and in this battle must have the alliance of the
patriarchal forces. But when this battle has been accomplished in
the culture, when the patriarchate has come to power, there is a
shift. The fathers, no longer in the service of human development,
become bearers of the authority complex. The mother, representing the supremacy of the unconscious, has become negative and assumes the character of dragon, Terrible Mother, the blind
instinctual forces that must be surpassed. The father figures are at
first the carriers of "heaven," the power to overcome the Great
Mother in her instinctual form, but once the Hero is committed to
win this dragon battle, the father begins to represent the negative
aspect of law and order, of duty, coercion, and prohibition—the
negative aspects of culture. In this way the father pays allegiance to
the Terrible Mother in her opposition to the Creator God, who is
doing the new thing, i.e., advancing consciousness. In Egypt the
maternal uncle was the bearer of this negative authority, but in
Israel the priesthood did so. Psychologically, it is not rivalry for the
mother that is involved in the "killing of the father," but the overcoming of the oppressive authority of the conscience created by the
patriarchy, the fathers. It is the authoritarian side of the father
archetype, which in Israel was projected upon the priestly leaders
and the law, that must be overcome. In every case there must be

an encounter with the carrier of this oppressive factor, for without the "murder of the 'father'," no development of consciousness and personality is possible.[13]

We must distinguish the two aspects, or forms, of the Terrible Father. He appears as the phallic Earth Father and as the frightening Spirit Father. Whenever the ego is overwhelmed by instinctual forces (e.g., sexual desires, aggressive or power drives, or any form of instinct), we see the work of the Terrible Mother. The phallic Terrible Father is really only the satellite of this Terrible Mother, not a masculine principle of equal importance. The other side of the Terrible Father is spiritual: from above and beyond, by not letting the son achieve self-fulfillment and victory, he captures and destroys the son's consciousness. This spiritual Terrible Father works through the forces of the old religion, the binding force of law, the old morality and the old order, all imposed with the coercion of conscience through the power of convention, education, and tradition. Any spiritual phenomenon that seizes the soul and obstructs its progress into a higher state of development may be the weapon of this Terrible Father.

> Any content that functions through its emotional dynamisms, such as the paralyzing grip of inertia or an invasion by instinct, belongs to the sphere of the mother, to nature. But all contents capable of conscious realization, a value, an idea, a moral canon, or some other spiritual force, are related to the father.[14]

Neumann observes that there are two forms of patriarchal castration (*castration* is always used metaphorically by Neumann): captivity and possession. "In captivity, the ego remains totally dependent upon the father as the representative of collective norms. . . . It remains bound by traditional morality and conscience, and, as though castrated by convention, loses the higher half of its dual nature."[15] The other form of patriarchal castration comes about if the son identifies with the father God; this form is possession and creates ego-inflation. The Ego-Hero loses contact with his earthly part, finitude, becomes lost in overweening pride, and will inevitably fall victim to the transpersonal powers that he is flaunting.

For the first form, captivity, Neumann coins the term *Isaac complex*. Isaac, relying utterly upon his father, does not stand on his own two feet. Furthermore, his religious experience is one of fear and trembling, i.e., dread. Excessive respect for the law, the authority of the collective father, drowns out the inner voice that announces the new manifestation of the divine. For these fathers' sons, the

> hero-bearing goddess is blotted out by the Terrible Father. They live entirely on the conscious plane and are incarcerated in a kind of spiritual uterus that never allows them to reach the fruitful feminine side of themselves, the creative unconscious. . . . The heroism that has been stifled in them manifests itself as sterile conservatism and a reactionary identification with the father, which lacks the living, dialectical struggle between the generations.[16]

The task of the Hero is not only to win the battle against the Mother and Father dragons but to set free the captive—"lonely Israel who mourns in exile here." Mythologically, the Hero, through his acts of valor, sets free the captive feminine (a princess, for example) and founds a new kingdom. We have seen the beginning of this process in Jesus' acts and proclamations in the synagogue and in his battle with the unclean spirit in the synagogue. An even more conclusive battle is Jesus' cleansing of the temple at Jerusalem. It is necessary now to try to understand the cleansing as the liberation of an aspect of Israel that in myth in general is depicted as liberation of slumbering or enchained womanhood. The essential quality of the feminine is *Eros*, which Jung defines as relatedness, or the ability to relate things and persons. In a man the quality of Eros manifests itself through his contrasexual side, his anima. Although Jung left the conception of Eros somewhat ambiguous, he was clear about its importance in the psyche both for men and for women. The Eros principle provides the attraction to things and people without which the psyche could not operate. All of us are acquainted with the power of love to motivate, to relate, and it was this kind of power that Jung associated with the dominant side of woman and the contrasexual side of man.

Certainly Judaism had lost this quality by emphasizing doctrinal and ritual purity and by demanding obedience to the law as the supreme religious virtue. Historically, Israel had evidenced a polarity between an emphasis on legal and doctrinal purity and a hungering for God, an abounding love of God. Into this tension Jesus came, and the first-century church viewed the tension polemically; thus, it highlighted one side as the enemy, which then became the target of its projected Shadow.

Archetypally, Israel had been captivated by a dominant patriarchal pattern and had repressed its feminine side; in this sense it was loveless. This masculine principle, which Jung called Logos, is found in both men and women; it is associated with consciousness, work, and achievement, especially with conscious understanding and discrimination. In practice (or, more accurately, in life) both principles are necessary; if either is missing or overly weak, the life of the individual or the community will suffer accordingly. As represented in the Old Testament books of Ruth, Hosea, and Jonah, a self-critical element was actively at work in Israel, testifying to the spiritual danger of stiff-necked pride, lack of love, and communal self-centeredness—perversions of Israel's basic covenant with God.

Perhaps because the newly born church had become clear about the matter of God's election to love and service rather than to glory, it read Israel's history and prophetic testimony as saying that Israel had persistently misunderstood her calling and refused her vocation. So both the Terrible Mother and the Terrible Father must be slain, i.e., transcended. According to the Apostle Paul, this was the reason that Israel was cut down and a wild olive branch, the Christians, grafted onto the tree. Jesus as Hero would be bound to undertake to deliver Israel, his bride-to-be, from her captivity to the patriarch of the priesthood and the law, the rulers of her lovelessness.

As the unconscious, the feminine side of the human is also the source of creativity and novelty. Israel's alienation from her own feminine depths was also symbolically attested by the lack of prophecy. For some four hundred years before Jesus, the voice of prophecy had been stilled in Israel. Israel had lost its creative union with God; she awaited a new day when the ministry of God's Spirit (fem-

inine in the Old Testament) would again cause her young men to
see visions and her old men to dream dreams.[17] Jesus spoke with
authority and taught new things, not as the scribes and rabbis, who
simply repeated what they had been taught, who stayed with "the
Book." Jesus, as Hero, has already been supported by the indwelling Spirit in his forty days' temptation and in his conflicts in the
synagogues. At this juncture the Spirit constrains him to go to Jerusalem. All the Synoptic Gospels place the event that concerns us
just after Jesus' triumphal entry into Jerusalem, during which he
was greeted by happy throngs, who placed palm branches in his
path and sang, "Hosanna! Blessed be he who comes in the name of
the Lord!" clearly implying that Jesus is somehow a new king for
the Jews. The Synoptics also note that it was Passover. Passover
was the time to remember and reenact in ritual the night of deliverance from Egypt, thus to remember Israel's purpose, her election.
The universal intent of God's love had been made clear to Israel
from the beginnings of the Exodus. In the second giving of the
Commandments, we find this appeal to Israel:

> "Circumcise therefore the foreskin of your heart, and be no longer stub-
> born. For the LORD your God is God of gods and LORD of lords, the
> great, the mighty, and the terrible God, who is not partial and takes no
> bribe. He executes justice for the fatherless and the widow, and loves
> the sojourner, giving him food and clothing. Love the sojourner there-
> fore; for you were sojourners in the land of Egypt."(Deut. 10:16–19)

Even in this recasting of the law many years after Moses, it is clear
that God has wider interests than Israel. But alas, even at this early
stage, the message was often overshadowed by the notion that
Israel was chosen for special favor to the exclusion of all others.

The great prophet Isaiah was clear about God's intent for Israel
and for her supreme place of worship. In a moving passage Isaiah
writes:

> Let not the foreigner who has joined himself to the LORD say,
>   "The LORD will surely separate me from his people";
> and let not the eunuch say,
>   "Behold, I am a dry tree."
> For thus says the LORD:
> "To the eunuchs who keep my sabbaths,

who choose the things that please me
and hold fast my covenant,
I will give in my house and within my walls
a monument and a name
better than sons and daughters;
I will give them an everlasting name
which shall not be cut off.

"And the foreigners who join themselves to the LORD,
to minister to him, to love the name of the LORD,
and to be his servants,
every one who keeps the sabbath, and does not profane it,
and holds fast my covenant—
these I will bring to my holy mountain,
and make them joyful in my house of prayer;
their burnt offerings and their sacrifices
will be accepted on my altar;
for my house shall be called a house of prayer
for all peoples." (Isa. 56:3–7)

It is apparent that Jesus agreed with Isaiah's sentiment that the temple was to be "a house of prayer for all peoples." His visit to the temple at this Passover is tantamount to a new exodus from Pharisaic Judaism, which had claimed God's gracious love only for itself and had excluded the stranger, the Gentile. The scene for this action of Jesus was that portion of the temple called the court of the Gentiles, an outer courtyard set aside for worship by the Gentiles, for those who might become proselytes of the God of Israel.

The court of the Gentiles was separated by a high partitioning wall from the holier parts of the Temple, and the court itself was regarded as having little sacred significance. It was a wide enclosure giving access to the interior parts of the building, but it was part of the Temple, and as such, fell under certain regulations. No one was to pass through it with dusty feet, or use it as a thoroughfare, and the use of it by the sick was forbidden. Because it was convenient and quite large, the sale of sacrificial beasts was licensed and allowed by the high priest, as was the exchanging of Roman coins of the worshipers for Temple shekels, the only acceptable mint for annual tribute, etc. There seems little doubt that this was a profitable business for the chief priest, but it was, nevertheless, a great convenience to the traveler, faced with the necessity, otherwise, of hauling sacrificial animals with him.

The buying and selling of sacrificial animals was not inherently evil, and it was not merely the commerce that was attacked by Jesus. Note that Mark says he "would not allow any one to carry anything through the temple" (ch. 11:16); i.e., he would not allow the use of the court for a shortcut. He was opposing the misuse of this court.[18]

Jesus' protest was against the priests who had made the temple a "den of thieves" by stealing for themselves exclusively the right of the Gentiles to know God. As Isaiah stated it,

> The dogs have a mighty appetite;
>   they never have enough.
> The shepherds also have no understanding;
>   they have all turned to their own way,
>   each to his own gain, one and all.

Jesus paid no attention to the Jewish ritual at the temple but focused his attention upon the rights of the Gentiles. This ignoring of the Jewish practices of worship might imply that the priesthood was no longer important in his sight. It was Jesus' view, as the New Testament presents it, that the whole temple had been corrupted by the desecration of the outer court. It was clear that the priesthood paid little attention to the injunction that the temple was to be a "house of prayer for all nations," nor had they cared to heed the prophecy of Zechariah concerning the day of the Lord—"there shall no longer be a trader in the house of the LORD of hosts on that day" (Zech. 14:21).

Jesus as Hero has the knowledge that "I and the Father are one," and is graced by the indwelling feminine spirit who teaches him in all things. Secure in these foundations, Jesus is empowered to be the Hero, to attack the dragon in its stronghold and expect victory over the powers of evil. Jesus dares to teach a new way. The Torah and the tradition of the elders have been warped by Pharisaic Judaism into something that, instead of helping spiritual growth and piety, in fact, prevents it. The dragon forces, secure in the seat of power, are using their power to keep others under control, dependent. In this myth, mother society has become the Terrible Mother and, in league with the Terrible Father, represents the Great Dragon, who destroys by ensnaring and enslaving.

In Jesus' time, in Israel, the dragon force that opposed spiritual development was the tradition-bound system of coercive, oppressive law and order, which could not manifest the new life it was intended to nurture. Neumann observes that "the adaptation of the individual to the collective, in disregard of his own needs not only castrates the individual but also endangers the community, for such unreserved adaptation to the collective transforms men into the components of a mass and . . . makes them a prey to every conceivable mass psychosis."[19] It is the battle against this dragon order that Jesus as Hero has now undertaken to free the princess Israel from captivity.

IX

The Sacred Marriage of the Hero

THE HERO as archetypal figure represents the destiny of psyche, of the soul. As "Son of God" this archetype is peculiarly related to the Self, the center and circumference of the psyche, the God archetype. It was, by the way, Jung's conviction that there was no way for psychology to differentiate between the God archetype and God. Thus, the Hero pioneers the way of the ego back to its proper connection with God. In the story of Jesus the final acts of this way involve two steps, or perhaps three, depending on how one divides the movements. The first is his death by crucifixion. The second is his resurrection and ascension, or resurrection-ascension.

In the preceding chapter I referred to the Hero's work of killing the tyrant dragon that is strangling culture and of winning the princess Israel as his bride. In myth the motif of the Sacred Marriage is prominent in the story of the Hero. This marriage represents the Hero's full integration of the psyche. "We live, most of us, utilizing only a small fraction of the energy that would be available to us were we not conflicted much of the time between the needs of the unconscious and the desires and wants that taunt our conscious hours."[1] Getting beyond this inner division is the last important step of the Hero journey toward final reunion with the God-center. The necessary prelude to the Sacred Marriage is the separation and discrimination that has been accomplished in the various steps of the journey already described. Without these, union would be unconscious, and without the reunion, life remains caught in opposition and warfare, or "the dull content, or discontent, of a half life where the mind ignores the heart or the heart is unconscious of meaning, even the meaning of love itself."[2] So long as one has not discovered, accepted, and related to the inner contrasexual side of one's psyche, there is a sense of incompleteness; the completion is sought outside, in another person, who can fill the empty spaces. This search for completion may take the form of sexual adventures, the procreation of many children, wallowing in the pleasures of the flesh, seeking security through money or other institutions, or, in Freud's sense, finding a way to give up responsibility and "return to the womb." It may also take the form of a marriage in which all the inner, lost values are projected onto the partner, who is then expected to live them out in the union.

The implicit longing in all these searches is for the missing half. For mythology this situation, or rather its resolution, is the Sacred Marriage, a form of the night-sea journey. Marriage is often connected with death, the ego's dissolving itself in the Mother unconscious.

The Easter events occupy a significant portion of each of the Gospels and contain a veritable forest of symbols. The following account does not attempt to do justice to that symbolic wealth but to single out the symbols that seem most important for the understanding of Jesus as Hero figure. Classically, this period is considered to begin with Jesus' entry into Jerusalem. The city itself was the queen city of Israel and the site of its symbolic religious center, the temple. It is probable that Mount Zion, a sacred site, was the location of the temple. Zion was David's royal city.

Jesus' entry into Jerusalem was no ordinary event, according to the story, but the coming of the Hero king to take charge of his kingdom. As was the custom for the king's coronation in Israel, he came in a royal procession, riding on a colt that had never before been ridden. The disciples who fetched the colt at Jesus' instruction threw their garments over it as a blanket-saddle.

> And many spread their garments on the road, and others spread leafy
> branches which they had cut from the fields. And those who went
> before and those who followed cried out, "Hosanna! Blessed is he who
> comes in the name of the Lord! Blessed is the kingdom of our father
> David that is coming! Hosanna in the highest!" (Mark 11:8–10)

Luke sharpens the meaning, saying, "Blessed be the King who
comes in the name of the Lord!" (Luke 19:38).

Commentators have generally agreed that this description is intended to parallel the coronation customs of Israel. The animal, as
was customary in the ancient world, had to be unbroken to be used
for sacred purposes. The cry "Hosanna," which means "save now,"
is in the hallel (Ps. 118:25), which was sung both at Passover and at
the Feast of Tabernacles. The word could be addressed to a king or
to God on behalf of a king. Psalm 118 comes from the temple and
may have been used at least in part, at coronations. The church has
used it consistently as a messianic psalm, presuming that it refers to
the coming of Jesus as King-Messiah.

What can all this mean archetypically? When we connect these
events with the myth of the Sacred Marriage, another set of meanings emerges. Jesus as King is entering the sacred queen city; the
king is making entry to the queen. The sexual reference may seem
farfetched, but double entendres are common in myth. Through
the Sacred Marriage the continued life of the world is guaranteed.
In this marriage, which in the oldest mythologies was celebrated
and consummated at the New Year festival, immediately after the
defeat of the dragon, the Hero embodies the Father archetype and
the bride embodies the fruitful side of the Mother archetype.[3] The
Hero unites himself with the woman he has set free by overcoming
the dragon and founds his kingdom with her.

In myth, as in the Gospel stories, the captive maiden is not an
individual: she represents the anima, the creative feminine, "the
treasure hard to attain" (i.e., the captive herself is the treasure).
Only the freeing and the marriage with this aspect of psyche allows,
or enables, the full creativity of psyche to proceed. Israel, we may
recall, was for four hundred years without prophecy, certainly an
evidence of her sterility. Liberating the captive and gaining the
treasure restores the connection with the Divine Center, the con-

crete evidence of which is the gift of the Holy Spirit to Jesus' disciples. This Spirit is to be an *indwelling*, not experienced as something outside and alien. The primordial creative powers, which in the creation myths were projected upon the cosmos, are now experienced as belonging to the human, as the depth of psyche.

In myth, sexual intercourse is the primordial symbol of creativity and the production of new life. In the later stages of many mythologies the symbols become rationalized or covered over with anecdotal material because the older imagery is no longer approved or, sometimes no longer meaningful. Joseph Campbell discusses a rite of the Catholic Church, performed on Holy Saturday, that allows the old imagery to shine through if one looks closely.

> . . . after the blessing of the new fire [symbolizing new life], the blessing of the paschal candle, and the reading of the prophecies, the priest puts on a purple cope and, preceded by the processional cross, the candelabra, and the lighted blessed candle, goes to the baptismal font with his ministers and the clergy, while the following tract is sung: "As the hart panteth after the fountains of water, so my soul panteth after Thee, O God! when shall I come and appear before the face of God? My tears have been my bread day and night, while they say to me daily: Where is thy God?" (Psalm xli, 2–4; Douay).
>
> On arriving at the threshold of the baptistry, the priest pauses to offer up a prayer, then enters and blesses the water of the font, "to the end that a heavenly offspring, conceived by sanctification, may emerge from the immaculate womb of the divine font, reborn new creatures: and that all, however distinguished either by sex in body, or by age in time, may be brought forth to the same infancy by grace, their spiritual mother." He touches the water with his hand, and prays that it may be cleansed of the malice of Satan; makes the sign of the cross over the water; divides the water with his hand and throws some towards the four quarters of the world; breathes thrice upon the water in the form of a cross; then dips the paschal candle in the water and intones: "May the virtue of the Holy Ghost descend into all the water of this font." He withdraws the candle, sinks it back again to a greater depth, and repeats in a higher tone: "May the virtue of the Holy Ghost descend into all the water of this font." Again he withdraws the candle, and for the third time sinks it, to the bottom, repeating in a higher tone still: "May the virtue of the Holy Ghost descend into all the water of this font." Then

breathing thrice upon the water he goes on: "And make the whole substance of this water fruitful for regeneration." He then withdraws the candle from the water, and, after a few concluding prayers, the assistant priests sprinkle the people with the blessed water.

The female water spiritually fructified with the male fire of the Holy Ghost is the Christian counterpart of the water of transformation known to all systems of mythological imagery. This rite is a variant of the sacred marriage, which is the source-moment that generates and regenerates the world and man, precisely the mystery symbolized by the Hindu lingam. To enter into this font is to plunge into the mythological realm; to break the surface is to cross the threshold into the night-sea.[4]

This rite clearly grasps the regenerative nature of baptism and connects it with the sexual act and with God's work in Christ, but it does not refer explicitly to the divine marriage. Yet, as soon as we think in mythological terms, the marriage is clearly the implied antecedent of the regenerative aspect of baptism. Jesus spoke to Nicodemus these words,

"Truly, truly, I say to you, unless one is born anew, he cannot see the kingdom of God." Nicodemus said to him, "How can a man be born when he is old? Can he enter a second time into his mother's womb and be born?" Jesus answered "Truly, truly, I say to you, unless one is born of water and the Spirit, he cannot enter the kingdom of God." (John 3:3–5)

By his entry into Jerusalem, Jesus as King is entering into and consummating the sacred marriage, which will bring about rebirth, the continuation of life in the world. But as is true in the ancient rites told in myth, in this process the King must die, a sacrifice to ensure the continued fertility of the life process. But here, at the triumphal entry, the King is coming to claim his kingdom and make it possible. The sacrifice to come is only a premonition:

"Behold, we are going up to Jerusalem; and the Son of man will be delivered to the chief priests and the scribes, and they will condemn him to death, and deliver him to the Gentiles; and they will mock him, and spit upon him, and scourge him, and kill him; and after three days he will rise." (Mark 10:33–34)

After the entry on Palm Sunday, as they come from Bethany on Monday, there is the puzzling but prophetic episode in which Jesus curses the barren fig tree: "May no one ever eat fruit from you again" (Mark 11:14). One of the meanings of *Bethany* is "house (place) of unripe figs," and the fig tree puts forth its first fruit on old branches before the leaves appear. This tree was fully leafed but without figs. Such a tree will not bear fruit. This fig tree is a symbol in the Gospels of the plight of Israel, its barrenness. In mythology the old, barren king must be replaced, and the new king will, of course, take his own queen-bride. The cleansing of the temple, which follows in the events of the story, has already been discussed, but it is perhaps the mythological equivalent of the overthrow of the old king and his barren regime. This old king, as represented by Israel's patriarchy, was alienated from the feminine. The psyche, which is alienated because its ego has been split apart from the ground of the feminine unconscious, is barren.

June Singer tells us that there "still remains in Jewish tradition a completely worldly way of experiencing the divine mysteries of the sacred marriage." The fact that the ritual custom of the Sabbath originated in mythic thought has mostly been forgotten. "Only vaguely, if at all, is it remembered that the family gathers to mark the holy union of God, the Most High, with his Heavenly Wisdom, the *Shekhinah*." But the marriage theme is present, for the sabbath is referred to as a bride celebrated in her union with Jacob, the patriarch of Israel. The wife prepares a special meal for her husband, and wine is served. "After the spiritual union has been consummated by each one, husband and wife, in themselves, the two are ready to enter into sexual union with one another. . . . It is incumbent on the husband and wife to have intercourse on the Sabbath." By so doing, they not only fulfill themselves but participate in the ancient mythic rite by which the world is recreated.[5]

In Mark 14:12 we read, "And on the first day of Unleavened Bread, when they sacrificed the passover lamb. . . ." Jesus was soon to be known as the Lamb of God sacrificed for the sin of the world. The lamb, a symbol of innocence, sweetness, forgiveness, and meekness, had a prominent role in Israel's sacrificial system, but nowhere more central than in the Passover rites. The Hero Jesus is clearly identified as the new gift of God, as was the ram that replaced Abraham's attempted offering of Isaac. This Lamb of God is to be sacrificed in the marriage rite as were the sons-lovers of old myth. In Revelation 19:6–7 we read:

> "Hallelujah! For the Lord our God the Almighty reigns.
> Let us rejoice and exult and give him the glory,
> for the marriage of the Lamb has come,
> and his Bride has made herself ready."

Revelation 21:9–10 identify this bride:

> "Come, I will show you the Bride, the wife of the Lamb." And in the Spirit he carried me away to a great, high mountain, and showed me the holy city Jerusalem coming down out of heaven from God.

The Hero, however, must not have his life taken from him involuntarily, as did an animal sacrificed in a renewal rite. Further, his sacrifice has to do with the feminine; it is an essential element of the rite of the sacred marriage. Rather than trying to understand the full meaning here, let us examine the further elements of this Jesus-Hero story, recalling that we are trying to understand this as the story of the individuating ego on its pilgrimage of soul making.

An important clue to the meaning of the events in Jesus' story is contained in the parable of the wicked husbandmen. The setting is the response to a question put to Jesus as he taught in the temple, a question put by the leaders of the patriarchal tyranny of the mythic story, i.e., the chief priests, scribes, and elders. These figures symbolize the masculinized ego-consciousness, dominated by its own rationality and enslaved by the legal system that it has created. Their question is this: "By what authority are you doing these things, or who gave you the authority to do them?" (Mark 11:27). The people who ask this question are those who have either failed or not even undertaken the second dragon battle; they are still involved in the problem of the First Parents, i.e., with the parental archetypes. As Neumann observes:

> To get stuck in this conflict and to yield to its fascination is characteristic of a large group of neurotics, and also of a certain spiritual type of man whose limitations lie precisely in his failure to master the feminine psyche in his fight with the dragon. . . .
> . . . The fact that they have failed to rescue and redeem the femi-

nine side of themselves is often expressed psychologically in an intensive preoccupation with universals to the exclusion of the personal, human element. Their heroic and idealistic concern with humanity at large lacks the self-limitation of the lover, who is ready to cleave to the individual and not to mankind and the universe alone. . . .

. . . Their manifest lack of feminine relationship is compensated by an excessively strong unconscious tie to the Great Mother. The non-liberation of the captive expresses itself in the continued dominance of the Great Mother under her deadly aspect, and the final result is alienation from the body and from the earth, hatred of life, and world negation.[6]

Remember that the legal system of late Judaism was set in motion by the work of the priests, Ezra and Nehemiah, who were deathly afraid of the feminine, especially the aspects of the Great Mother that were represented in the Mother Goddesses of the ancient Near East. Patriarchy and the law became a bulwark against the feared excesses should there be any traffic with the feminine. This fear and consequent rigidity, however, create an ego system that is hostile to the unconscious. Although this may be a good and necessary step for the developing ego as it strives to be free of the destructive drives of the unconscious, as in the Oedipal struggle, this separation must be transcended. The bearers of authority in the patriarchate have become possessed by an authority complex. "For the hero who represents the new consciousness, the hostile dragon is the old order, the obsolete psychic stage which threatens to swallow him up again."[7] But the enemy is not the father, per se, i.e., not the personal father, nor ego-consciousness itself; the enemy is the negative aspect of the Father archetype, the Terrible Male. This figure is symbolized in matriarchal myth as the maternal uncle, the bearer of authority. It is authority that is rigid, that results in the frustration of personal responsibility and thus of ego development. This system appears as the binding forces of the old law, religion, morality, as superego/conscience, convention, tradition, or any other cultural phenomenon that blocks the progress of soul making at this junction.[8]

In this light, the parable that Jesus tells in response to the question about authority takes on clear meaning.

"A man planted a vineyard, and set a hedge around it, and dug a pit for the wine press, and built a tower, and let it out to tenants, and went into another country. When the time came, he sent a servant to the tenants, to get from them some of the fruit of the vineyard. And they took him and beat him, and sent him away empty-handed. Again he sent to them another servant, and they wounded him in the head, and treated him shamefully. And he sent another, and him they killed; and so with many others, some they beat and some they killed. He had still one other, a beloved son; finally he sent him to them, saying, 'They will respect my son.' But those tenants said to one another. 'This is the heir; come, let us kill him, and the inheritance will be ours.' And they took him and killed him, and cast him out of the vineyard. What will the owner of the vineyard do? He will come and destroy the tenants, and give the vineyard to others." (Mark 12:1–9)

The ego that proclaims itself the master of its own soul or the ego that is enslaved to an authoritative tradition experiences the plight of the wicked husbandmen. The ego has taken control of the psyche and is no longer in communication with the deeper forces, the creative aspect of the psyche; it is cut off from the unconscious and hence from the Divine Center. The Hero, by overcoming for himself (and later for his society) the authoritarian forces, the tyranny of the elders and the past, opens the way to a new period of creativity.

In preparing his disciples for the final phases of his self-sacrifice, Jesus shares with them a supper that has become the model for the central rite of the church.

And as they were eating, he took bread, and blessed, and broke it, and gave it to them, and said, "Take; this is my body." And he took a cup, and when he had given thanks he gave it to them, and they all drank of it. And he said to them, "This is my blood of the covenant, which is poured out for many." (Mark 14:22–24)

For the church, and hence for the story we are following, this rite became not a Passover meal, but the replacement for the Passover meal and was thought to have occurred "on the night when Jesus was betrayed."

The principal elements of the rite are bread and wine. That the bread, according to Mark's account, was leavened bread implies, as does the wine, a transforming element. Jesus' words identify the broken bread with his body and the wine with his blood. The killing and eating of a person identified as a god is an ancient mythological rite, often celebrated in all too real blood and flesh. Campbell relates such an event from Dutch South New Guinea in connection with a puberty rite. At the termination of the rite a boy and a girl who have engaged in public ritual coitus are killed, cut up, roasted, and eaten.[9] Such rites, Campbell indicates, make visible the mythological forces themselves. "For the festival is an extension into the present of the world-creating mythological event through which the force of the ancestors (those eternal ones of the dream) became discharged into the rolling run of time, and where what then was ever present in the form of a holy being without change now dies and reappears, dies and reappears—like the moon, like the yam, like our animal food, or like the race. The divine being has become flesh in the living food-substance of the world."[10]

Passover, by its dating, was and is both a lunar festival and a solar festival. In Old Testament history it commemorates the Exodus, but its date is that of the full moon of the spring equinox. This date is also that of two ancient festivals—an agricultural and a shepherding festival. The firstlings of the lambs were to be sacrificed on this date, and a wave offering of the first of the barley harvest was offered the following morning. The lunar dating tells us that we are in the realm of the Mother Goddess and mythologies. In that realm, creation and its renewal "cannot take place except from *a living being who is immolated*—a primordial androgynous giant, or a cosmic Male, or a Mother goddess or a mythic Young Woman." The ancient idea was that life could spring only from another life that had been sacrificed. The life in that one sacrificed person, particularly a divine person, overflows and manifests itself on the cosmic or collective scale, so that a single being is multiply reborn in a whole group. "Here again we find the well-known cosmogonic pattern of the primordial 'wholeness' broken into fragments by the act of Creation."[11] Do we not hear echoes of this archetypal symbolism in Jesus' words "This is my body broken for you," and "I am the bread of life"?

Although Jesus is the "Lamb of God," hence identified with the shepherding tradition, the symbols of this supper with his disciples—wheat (bread) and the grape (wine) seem to connect the rite with vegetation mythology. In the myths of vegetation people, the spirit of grain is commonly represented in animal form, as it is in the lamb.

A redemptive element in the mystique of agriculture is also present in the rite of Jesus' meal with his disciples. Eliade observes that

> . . . plant life, which is reborn by means of apparent disappearance (the burying of seed in the earth) offers at once an example and a hope; the same thing may happen to the souls of the dead. . . . Agriculture [i.e., reflection upon it] taught man the fundamental oneness of organic life; and from that revelation sprang the simpler analogies between woman and field, between the sexual act and sowing, as well as the most advanced intellectual syntheses: life as rhythmic, death as a return, and so on.[12]

The ear or sheaf of grain is an "emblem of fertility and an attribute of the sun. It also symbolizes the idea of germination and growth, the development of any feasible potentiality. . . . Loaves [of bread] are symbols of fecundity and perpetuation, which is why they sometimes take on forms that are sexual in implication."[13]

Although the symbols of bread and wine are agricultural, the wine, especially red wine, is symbolic of sacrifice and of blood. Wine, like the god most connected with it—Dionysus, or Bacchus—is an ambivalent symbol, meaning both blood and sacrifice but also youth and eternal life, such as the divine intoxication of the soul hymned by Greek and Persian poets, which enables one to partake for a fleeting moment of the mode of being attributed to the gods. Dionysus was originally a god of vegetation, a son-lover god who died and was resurrected yearly in the liturgy of the Great Mother Goddess. His cult observance was one of death and dismemberment and resurrection. But wine also means blood, the blood of sacrifice, which connects it symbolically with the tradition of the hunting peoples and their shaman visionaries. Blood is the most precious sacrifice of all, for it means that the life principle itself is being given up to the god. Each ritual sacrifice reenacts the primordial sacrifice by which the world was created. The ancients believed that no creation can occur without sacrifice. To sacrifice what is dear is to sacrifice oneself, and the spiritual energy thereby acquired is proportional to the importance of what has been lost.

The rite of killing the firstborn of flocks and fields in the planting cultures stems from the myth of the divine being who had become flesh in the living food substance of the world, in all of us. This god, in the beginning, had, through death, brought into being all the plants. Another part of their myth was that plants are like the moon, dying and being reborn in a regular cycle. The rites of sacrifice teach the immortality of being, and the individual is, through the rite, united with that being, thus transcending death and becoming reconciled to a world in which life feeds upon death. The rite is a fresh reenactment of the god's own sacrifice in the beginning. In the mythic rite, time is transcended or transformed so that the time of the beginning is here and now. Thus, among the planting peoples the cycles of nature and of the moon became the locus of an archetypal projection, the symbols of the archetype of renewal. Recall that apparently we recognize in the outer world only (at least, at first) that which symbolizes the archetypal realities that reign over us. Behind the seeming monstrosity of the universe in which life feeds upon death, a greater truth lies in wait, the truth of the self-giving deity who is "in, with and under" the whole mysterious play of things and beings, who thus numbers the very hairs of our heads and without whose awareness not so much as a sparrow falls to the ground.

Human sacrifice, and by extension, certain notions of the Christian mass, can best be understood as variations of the mythologem of the divine being who was killed and planted to become the food of humanity. Archetypal truths, it seems, must also struggle to reach a high level of consciousness and clarity; all too easily, they fall victim to literalization on the plane of history. For the archetype presents itself only in symbolic dress, and every symbol is multivalent, subject to growth in insight by the very consciousness it fosters. But how is this archetypal insight realized?

How did the greater myth—the myth of the eternal return—come to be? Perhaps the best clue lies in the tradition of the shaman and his visionary capacity. The way of the planting peoples led to villages, an organized priesthood, law and order, tradition and

society. The way of the hunting peoples led to the development of
the individual, of courage, initiative, creativity, and independence,
but above all, to the vision quest, from which came novelty and insight into a superior order. An old chieftain of the Ogallalla Sioux
told Natalie Curtis, "From Wakan-Tanka, the Great Mystery,
comes all power," and he continued:

> It is from Wakan-Tanka that the Holy Man has wisdom and the power
> to heal and to make holy charms. Man knows that all healing plants are
> given by Wakan-Tanka; therefore are they holy. So too is the buffalo
> holy, because it is the gift of Wakan-Tanka. The Great Mystery gave to
> men all things for their food, their clothing, and their welfare. And to
> man he gave also the knowledge how to use these gifts—how to find the
> holy healing plants, how to hunt and surround the buffalo, how to
> know wisdom. For all comes from Wakan-Tanka—all.
>
> To the Holy Man comes in youth the knowledge that he will be
> holy. The Great Mystery makes him to know this. Sometimes it is the
> Spirits who tell him. The Spirits come not in sleep always, but also
> when man is awake. When a Spirit comes it would seem as though a
> man stood there, but when this man has spoken and goes forth again,
> none may see whither he goes. Thus the Spirits. With the Spirits the
> Holy Man may commune always, and they teach him holy things.
>
> The Holy Man goes apart to a lone tipi and fasts and prays. Or he
> goes into the hills in solitude. When he returns to men, he teaches
> them and tells them what the Great Mystery has bidden him to tell. He
> counsels, he heals, and he makes holy charms to protect the people
> from all evil. Great is his power and greatly is he revered; his place in
> the tipi is an honored one.[14]

Insights such as these, the messages of the spirits, are received
or incorporated in mythic form and then told and retold. Jesus'
forty days of temptation in the wilderness would seem a clear
equivalent of the shaman's vision quest, and his repeated retreats
for prayer and fasting suggest his communing with the spirit so that
he could be taught holy things. It is from the last of these prayer-
fasts in the garden of Gethsemane that he comes forth to go to his
death, "nevertheless not my will, but thine, be done" (Luke 22:42).

It is also in the tradition of the shaman that the miraculous phenomena are rooted. In their rites of initiation and in their healing
practices, shamans experienced events much like the miracles of the
Gospels, miracles of healing, of resurrection of the dead, and of con-

trol over nature, the power that Jesus showed in stilling the storm and casting out the demon powers. Here, too, is more than a hint of the founding of mythic insight into the mental crisis that is the initiation of the shaman. And as Campbell observes, "the shamanistic crisis, when properly fostered yields an adult not only of superior intelligence and refinement, but also of greater physical stamina and vitality of spirit than is normal to the members of his group."[15] The shaman's initiation is invariably a death and resurrection experience. After his initiation the shaman is stronger than death.

Through his trance the shaman learned how to reach the mythological realm, the depth of psyche; the results were the gifts of the Great Spirit—food, healing, and the arts. But it is also likely the shaman who discovered individual immortality as opposed to the communal, or species, immortality of the planters. The planter's view is based on the notion of group participation, of collectivity as the final truth about life. The hunter's is based on the thought that immortality is a property, not just of the group, but of the individual. The hunting peoples sensed that an immortal individual inhabited each person. The shaman, after he dies in the initiatory rite, comes back a changed person but also the same person. Probably from the shamans arose the idea that a person was the manifestation of a god. As is true in the ritual of contemporary primitives, when the human is enveloped in sacred attire and performing in a sacred ritual, he becomes more than a representation of the divine—he is the present manifestation of the divine and a conduit of divine power, therefore, taboo.[16]

What happens in the symbols of bread and wine of Jesus' last supper is the uniting and transcending of the myths of the hunters and of the planters. His is indeed a "new covenant," unknown not only in Israel but perhaps unknown anywhere else. Although the planting peoples are dominantly feminine and the hunters and shamans are dominantly masculine in mythology, both are necessary for the continued health and development of psyche. This theme will be explored in more detail through the Hero's passion, death, and resurrection.

From the complex narrative of Jesus' crucifixion, only a few of the events and symbols can be treated. First, the Hero, although betrayed, went of his own volition to his death. Having sensed the forthcoming betrayal and death, the Hero had prepared himself and his followers. His last preparation was a nightlong vigil of prayer in Gethsemane, from which he went to be handed over to the authorities. In the episode of his capture, he used his miraculous shamanistic powers one final time when he healed the soldier's ear, which had been severed by an overzealous disciple. At his trial before the authorities he was convicted of pretending to be a Messiah-King. "The high priest asked him, 'Are you the Christ, the Son of the Blessed?' And Jesus said, 'I am; and you will see the Son of man seated at the right hand of Power, and coming with the clouds of heaven" (Mark 14:61–62). Later, early in the morning, Jesus was delivered to Pilate by the chief priests. "And Pilate asked him, 'Are you the King of the Jews?' And he answered him, 'You have said so'" (Mark 15:2). Pilate wished to release Jesus, but the fierce intensity of the crowd's "Crucify him" persuaded Pilate to accede to their demands. After Jesus was tormented and mocked by the soldiers, saluted in jest as "King of the Jews," he was taken to be crucified. On a cross of wood he was crucified between two thieves. Tradition quickly recognized the cross as the "tree" and, of course, the place of crucifixion was *Golgotha*, meaning "skull," translated into Latin as *calvaria*, and into English as *Calvary*. The common understanding is that the place was so named because it was a promontory shaped like a skull. In the tradition, then, the crucifixion was quickly placed on a rude tree on the mountain called Calvary—in mythological symbolism, the tree and the mountain.

According to the tradition, Jesus had spoken of himself as the vine and his disciples as the branches. Vine, grape, and wine are closely associated with the Great Mother Goddess. Eliade tells us that in the Near East, the vine was identified with the "hub of life" and that the Sumerian sign for "life" was originally a vine leaf. The vine is sacred to the Great Goddess, who is often called the mother vine or the goddess vine. Further, she is often found at the "center of the world" beside the *omphalos*, the tree of life and the four springs. Among the planting cultures, the vine was the symbol of immortality, just as wine was the symbol of youth and everlasting life in primitive traditions. The Mishna teaches that the tree of knowledge of good and evil, in Genesis, was a vine. Grapes and wine symbolized wisdom until quite late in Old Testament tradition. All these associations of symbol in myth have a clear and powerful meaning: here on this mount, with this tree, we have a "center of the world," *axis mundi*, a source of life, youth, and immortality. The trees signify the universe in endless regeneration, but at the heart of the universe is always a tree, the tree of eternal life or knowledge.[17] In Christian legend and symbolism the cross is often depicted as the tree of life, able to bring the dead to life, and as made from the wood of the tree of life of the Garden of Eden.

In Mesopotamia a central hill called the mountain of the lands is believed to join the sky to the earth. It may well be that Tabor, the Palestinian mountain of tradition, started out as *tabbur*, meaning "navel", *omphalos*. Mount Gerizim was known as the navel of the earth. A common tradition is that Palestine was not covered by the flood because it was so high in elevation, near the summit of the cosmic mountain. To Christians, Golgotha became the center of the world; it was both the topmost point of the cosmic mountain and the spot where Adam was created and buried. The blood of Jesus was thus shed over Adam's skull at the very foot of the cross, and thus was Adam redeemed, transformed.[18]

Tree and water motifs are widely associated with the inexhaustible creative powers of deity, especially with the Mother Goddesses. The symbols water, tree, creation, and life are similarly associated both in Jewish and in Christian traditions. Ezekiel, chapter 47, describes a scene in which miraculous waters flow beneath the temple toward the east, a veritable river of life.

> "And wherever the river goes every living creature which swarms will live, and there will be very many fish. . . . And on the banks, on both sides of the river, there will grow all kinds of trees for food. Their leaves will not wither nor their fruit fail, but they will bear fresh fruit every month, because the water for them flows from the sanctuary. Their fruit will be for food, and their leaves for healing." (vss. 9–12)

Revelation 22:1–5 carries this same motif, connecting it with the Lamb.

The tree of crucifixion has been transformed in Christian legend into the tree of life. This tree is now the center of the world, the source of life and is appropriately located on the holy mountain. Medieval art in the Strasbourg Cathedral shows a cross growing from Adam's grave. A Christian legend says that Adam was buried on Golgotha and that Seth planted on his grave a twig from the paradisal tree. This tree grew to become the cross of Christ, the tree of death and of life. In many parts of the world, death is associated with a tree that has characteristics reminiscent of the two trees of the Garden of Eden. One side of the tree is green, living; the other is dead. The Eddic myth of Scandinavia includes the great ash tree Yggdrasil, at the axle of the world, its roots piercing the abyss and its top branches in the heavens, one of them shading Valhalla. But as its root the cosmic serpent gnaws, and four stags browse on its leaves.

> The ash Yggdrasil suffers anguish,
>   More than men can know:
> The stag bites above; on the side it rots;
> And the dragon gnaws from beneath.

The great god Odin hung on this tree nine days, a sacrifice to himself:

> I ween that I hung on the windy tree,
>   Hung there for nights full nine;
> With the spear I was wounded, and offered I was
>   To Odin, myself to myself,
> On that tree that none may ever know
>   What root beneath it runs.[19]

In this supreme initiation, death and life are shown as an inseparable pair, a polarity. The primal pair, Adam and Eve, brought both death and procreation into the world by their relationship to the two trees. Christ, the second Adam, by his death on this tree, brings eternal life.

> Then some of the scribes and Pharisees said to him, "Teacher, we wish to see a sign from you." But he answered them, "An evil and adulterous generation seeks for a sign; but no sign shall be given to it except

the sign of the prophet Jonah. For as Jonah was three days and three nights in the belly of the whale, so will the Son of man be three days and three nights in the heart of the earth." (Matt. 12:38–40)

In his discourse with Nicodemus, Jesus said, "Truly, truly, I say to you, unless one is born of water and the Spirit, he cannot enter the kingdom of God" (John 3:5). And later in the same discourse, "And as Moses lifted up the serpent in the wilderness, so must the Son of man be lifted up, that whoever believes in him may have eternal life" (John 3:14). Water is a universal symbol for the unconscious, i.e., for the Mother Goddess of the psyche. Moses' staff-serpent symbolism also connects us with the Mother Goddess. As the seat and source of transformation and renewal, the tree has a feminine and maternal significance.[20] A sixteenth-century engraving shows Christ on the cross as a tree in a garden. The tree bears every sort of fruit, and people are pulling down the branches to gather the fruit.[21] Jung observes that the logos nature of Christ is often represented by the chthonic serpent and is the maternal wisdom of the divine mother, prefigured by *Sapientia* (Wisdom) in the Old Testament. "The snake-symbol thus characterizes Christ as a personification of the unconscious in all its aspects, and as such he is hung on the tree in sacrifice ('wounded by the spear,' like Odin)."[22]

As in a shamanic initiation, Jesus, manifesting the sign of Jonah, is to die and descend to the underworld, there to remain until the third day, when he will rise again. Jonah's night-sea journey is modeled on the death and rebirth of the sun, which passes into the sea in the west at night, to be carried by boat across the waters of the underworld and reborn the following morning in the east. The shaman, remember, discovered a technique that made access to the mythological realm possible. The mythological realm is for us the unconscious; or at least, access is through the unconscious. In the ancient mythic world the universe in general was conceived as having three levels: sky, earth, and underworld—all connected by a central axis, often depicted as the world tree. The preeminently shamanic technique is the passage from one cosmic region to another. Among the Babylonians the link between heaven and earth is symbolized variously as a cosmic mountain or its replica—a temple, a ziggurat, a royal city or palace, sometimes imagined as a celestial column. Prayers and offerings could be sent up to the gods in the temples or by burning, the smoke from which rose to the heavens. But only the shaman could use the connection between earth and heaven for a concrete and personal ascent.[23] The notion of three communicating zones was by no means limited to one area of the world. Rather, it is a universal concept connected with belief in the possibility of direct communication with the sky. But for the shamans, this connection of communication is a concrete and personal experience that is ecstatic or mystical. "In other words, what for the rest of the community remains a cosmological ideogram, for the shamans (and the heroes, *etc.*) becomes a mystical itinerary."[24]

In the Gospel of Mark we read:

> And it was the third hour, when they crucified him. And the inscription of the charge against him read, "The King of the Jews." And with him they crucified two robbers, one on his right and one on his left. . . .
>
> And when the sixth hour had come, there was darkness over the whole land until the ninth hour. And at the ninth hour Jesus cried with a loud voice, "E´lo-i, E´lo-i, la´ma sabach-tha´ni?" which means "My God, my God, why hast thou forsaken me?" . . . And Jesus uttered a loud cry, and breathed his last. And the curtain of the temple was torn in two, from top to bottom. (Mark 15:25–38)

And as Matthew reports:

> . . . and the earth shook, and the rocks were split; the tombs also were opened, and many bodies of the saints who had fallen asleep were raised, and coming out of the tombs after his resurrection they went into the holy city and appeared to many. When the centurion and those who were with him, keeping watch over Jesus, saw the earthquake and what took place, they were filled with awe, and said, "Truly this was the Son of God!"
>
> There were also many women there, looking on from afar, who had followed Jesus from Galilee, ministering to him; among whom were Mary Magdalene, and Mary the mother of James and Joseph, and the mother of the sons of Zebedee.
>
> When it was evening, there came a rich man from Arimathea, named Joseph, who also was a disciple of Jesus. He went to Pilate and asked for the body of Jesus. Then Pilate ordered it to be given to him.

And Joseph took the body, and wrapped it in a clean linen shroud, and laid it in his own new tomb, which he had hewn in the rock; and he rolled a great stone to the door of the tomb, and departed. Mary Magdalene and the other Mary were there, sitting opposite the sepulchre. . . .

Now after the sabbath, toward the dawn of the first day of the week, Mary Magdalene and the other Mary went to see the sepulchre. And behold, there was a great earthquake; for an angel of the Lord descended from heaven and came and rolled back the stone, and sat upon it. His appearance was like lightning, and his raiment white as snow. And for fear of him the guards trembled and became like dead men. But the angel said to the women, "Do not be afraid; for I know that you seek Jesus who was crucified. He is not here; for he has risen, as he said. Come, see the place where he lay. Then go quickly and tell his disciples that he has risen from the dead, and behold, he is going before you to Galilee; there you will see him. Lo, I have told you." So they departed quickly from the tomb with fear and great joy, and ran to tell his disciples. And behold, Jesus met them and said, "Hail!" And they came up and took hold of his feet and worshiped him. Then Jesus said to them, "Do not be afraid; go and tell my brethren to go to Galilee, and there they will see me." . . .

Now the eleven disciples went to Galilee, to the mountain to which Jesus had directed them. And when they saw him they worshiped him; but some doubted. (Matt. 27:51—28:17)

Finally, the ending that is found in some but not all the more reliable manuscripts of the Gospel of Mark:

Now when he rose early on the first day of the week, he appeared first to Mary Magdalene, from whom he had cast out seven demons. She went out and told those who had been with him, as they mourned and wept. But when they heard that he was alive and had been seen by her, they would not believe it.

After this he appeared in another form to two of them, as they were walking into the country. And they went back and told the rest, but they did not believe them. . . .

Afterward he appeared to the eleven themselves as they sat at table; and he upbraided them for their unbelief and hardness of heart, because they had not believed those who saw him after he had risen. And he said to them, "Go into all the world and preach the gospel to the whole creation. He who believes and is baptized will be saved; but he who does not believe will be condemned. And these signs will accompany those who believe; in my name they will cast out demons; they will speak in new tongues; they will pick up serpents, and if they drink

any deadly thing, it will not hurt them; they will lay their hands on the
sick, and they will recover."

So then the Lord Jesus, after he had spoken to them, was taken up
into heaven, and sat down at the right hand of God. And they went
forth and preached everywhere, while the Lord worked with them and
confirmed the message by the signs that attended it. Amen. (Mark
16:9–20)

One of the more surprising things about these accounts of Jesus'
death and resurrection is that they are dominated by women. All
his disciples, save possibly the "beloved disciple," have fallen away
in fear; even Peter, that staunch "rock," has denied him three
times before cockcrow. Only the women remain; they are many,
and several are named. The importance of the feminine principle in
these last events of the Hero's life seems to be confirmed by the
emphasis on the women. We have ample reason to connect these
events with the ancient rites of renewal through the sacrificial
death of the king, or son-lover, of the Great Goddess and her symbolic water and serpent. Recall, also, that the king embodied not
only the life-principle of the Mother but the culture-principle of
the Father. He was an incarnation of the gods of life and culture.
Culture was connected with the fathers, the gods of the sky, usually
a solar deity, for the sun has an orderly, dependable cycle. The
mysterious life-principle was connected with the mothers, lunar
deities, for the light of the moon is changeable.

In the cycle of nature, which inspired the planting peoples'
myths, life is always followed by death, to be followed by rebirth.
This cycle is true of the myths of all the goddesses and their sons-
lovers and is figured in the heavens by the moon and the planet
Venus, which, as evening and morning star, are an image both for
night-sleep-death and for dawn-rebirth. The moon itself, like
Jonah, is three days in the dark, and then its renewal begins. And
the son-lover of the Great Goddess dies always to be reborn. But it
is through the agency of the Great Goddess that he dies and that he
lives again. A beautiful myth is the story of the goddess Inanna,
whose son-lover, Tammuz (Damuz), is the model for the kings of
the planting peoples' culture. For the son-lover relationship, we
might call to mind the madonna-and-child motif of Christian art and

tradition. After the death of her son, Inanna descends to the underworld and there is stripped of her queenly attributes; finally,
Inanna, the Queen of Heaven, stands naked before her sister,
Ereshkigal, the Queen of the Underworld, and the seven judges of
the underworld. "At their word . . . / The sick woman was turned
into a corpse, / And the corpse was hung from a stake. / After three
days and three nights had passed / Her messenger, Ninshubur, . . .
Filled the heaven with complaints for her." Ninshubur is also
known as the messenger of the gods and is a god of wings. He has
been directed to appeal to several other gods, most noteworthy of
whom is Enki, the Lord of Wisdom, who knows the food of life and
the water of life. Ninshubur is, of course, the earlier counterpart of
Hermes, the Olympian messenger of the gods and the guide of
souls to the underworld and to rebirth. Hermes' staff is the cadu-
ceus, with entwined serpents. The serpents connect us immediately again to the world of the renewing, ever-dying and reborn
serpent, who is the naked goddess in her serpent form.[25]

The myth further tells us that Enki, Lord of Wisdom and Lord of
the Waters of the Abyss, was troubled when he heard of the troubles
of his daughter and fashioned two sexless creatures (angels?). To one
he gave the water of life and to the other the food of life; he then
directed them to sprinkle each upon the corpse of Inanna sixty
times. Inanna arose and ascended from the nether world, and whoever had descended peacefully to the nether world hastened ahead
of her. This is the basic Sumerian version, but an important Babylo-
nian variant makes it clear that she goes to the underworld to rescue
her dead son, Tammuz. This myth exists in many versions—the
Mother Goddess and her son-lover, who dies to be resurrected—Isis
and Osiris, Cybele and Attis, Aphrodite and Adonis.

Mother Goddesses both destroy their loving victims and lovingly gather up their pieces and restore them to life and love. The
death of the sons-lovers is necessary because the old has grown
anemic by feeding only upon the goodness of the mother. Consider
"the beautiful Tammuz who is the yearly victim of his too-feminine
beauty and never achieves heroic stature as a man."[26] This necessary death is the yearly death of the king, sacrificed for the renewal
of the world. But Mother Goddesses are of the planting peoples,

and as the story of Cain and Abel has made clear, the Hebrews are not planters, and their God prefers a meaty sacrifice. Because of the Jewish prejudice against the feminine, the wisdom of the feminine was lost, or largely lost, to Israel and its exclusively masculine leadership. Nonetheless, the resistance to the feminine and to the cycle of renewal through death and rebirth demanded the something more that was to be forthcoming, a full connection with the Father God. Among the Jews this loss and this hope were projected into the desire for a King-Messiah who would deliver them, and we have noted the cry for deliverance that precedes the birth of the Hero. Their wish for deliverance and their intuition of its possibility became a longing for immortality that could not be fulfilled until the resurrection of the body reached its full potential in Jesus and the Christian myth. This Hero, however, does not connect merely with the Father, although he can say, "I and the Father are one"; he also connects with the Mother, nowhere more obviously than in his death, the sign of Jonah, three days and three nights in the depths, resurrection on the third day.

The king may also represent, in the economy of the psyche, the ego. As the king is the head of the state, so the ego is the head of the personality. In the shamanic tradition, the full range of the shaman's powers includes the ability to ascend to heaven via the *axis mundi*, the center, but also to descend to the netherworld via the same axis, his sacred pole, or tree. Jesus, lifted up on the tree, like Moses' serpent-staff in the wilderness, which protected the people against deadly bites and brought forth the lifegiving water from the rock, descends in Jonah's journey to the underworld of the Mother, to gain her renewing power. This shamanic ability to ascend and descend was no mere trick but a powerful rite of psychic initiation from which could and did emerge a new and transcendent consciousness. Jesus' resurrection, however, is more than the shaman was able to do. Jesus-Hero affirms that with him the universal has burst into time; the last age (the *eschaton*) has come. The eternal wheel of life, from which Buddha and his followers found escape, is here transcended in and through the resurrection of the body, not just rebirth into ordinary life, but into a transcendent life. Jesus is the "firstborn from the dead."

Yet we must ask, what is this mythic axis, this tree of life and death through which the energies of the universe pour, which connects the realm of the Mother and the realm of the Father, by which the shamans can ascend and descend and by which Christ descends and ascends? To ask what the axis is, is to ask for a shift in symbolism. The key we are following says that the symbols always refer to the adventure of psyche in its pilgrimage of soul making. Analytical psychologists have suggested that the axis connecting the ego with the central principle of the psyche, the Ego-Self axis, may well be the referent of the tree symbolism. Thus, tree symbolism may represent either a means by which psychic energy flows or the psychic energy itself. This tree is closely associated with the Mother Goddess, i.e., the unconscious aspect of psyche, who is the source of psychic energy but who also becomes at times a barrier to its flow. And the forms into which the energy is to flow are represented by the Father God, whose law may also become a barrier to the flow of energy.

Jesus, the Logos of the Father, is being united with the earth in his death, i.e., united first of all with *mater*, Mother Earth, who is also Sophia, the divine wisdom. As Logos, the Son is indeed the Father: "I and the Father are one." It is the union of the logos wisdom of the son-father with the Sophia wisdom of the mother-body that constitutes the mystical marriage within the psyche and thus frees the Holy Spirit. In his conversation with Nicodemus, Jesus indicated that to attain eternal life, one must be reborn of *water* and the *spirit*. In the mythological realm, water is a clear symbol for the Mother and she, as the *fons et origo*, the universal congress of potentialities, is also connected in symbol with the unconscious. In Genesis, God's Spirit hovers over the waters, and it is God's Spirit that impregnates the Virgin Mary in the Gospel stories. "Immersion in water signifies a return to the preformal state, with a sense of death and annihilation on the one hand, but of rebirth and regeneration on the other, since immersion intensifies the life-force." Cirlot also quotes St. John Chrysostom: "It represents death and interment, life and resurrection. . . . When we plunge our head beneath water, as in a sepulchre, the old man becomes completely immersed and buried. When we leave the water, the new man suddenly appears." Finally, Cirlot notes that water is an "expression of the vital potential of the psyche."[27] The ancient matriarchial understanding of renewal, the endless rebirth of life from death, is akin to this water symbolism. In the psyche, renewal is only possible by a descent into the unconscious, a return to the mother (see ch.7).

As noted, the myth of eternal return is not enough and is transcended in the Jesus-Hero myth. In his discussion with Nicodemus, Jesus says, "That which is born of the flesh is flesh, and that which is born of the Spirit is spirit" (John 3:6). In this same dialogue Jesus speaks of the necessity of his being lifted up, as Moses lifted the serpent in the wilderness, and of himself as the one who has descended from heaven and who ascends to heaven. The serpent motif refers clearly to the realm of the Mother Goddess, but in Moses' staff being lifted up to heaven and in Jesus' ascension, a connection is made with the realm of the Father God of heaven. In the joint connection with the Mother and the Father, the Jesus Hero story transcends the myths of the matrilineal and the patriarchal traditions of the shamans.

Death is the primordial symbol for the decay and dissolution of the personality, but in the Hero stories runs a countervailing force for the needed stability and indestructibility. Neumann observes twin dangers for the developing consciousness, in addition to the fight with the dragon—the fascination with the world and with the unconscious. One may easily get caught up in the "ten thousand" things of the world and lose the spiritual quest, but the inertial power of the unconscious is continually seeking to lure consciousness back into its depths. "Magic and religion, art, science, and technics are man's creative efforts to cope with this threat on two fronts."[28] The goal is stability and indestructibility, which have their mythological prototype in the conquest of death.

It is Neumann's conviction that the Osiris myth of Egypt can shed considerable light upon the meaning of the Hero's death for the needed stability and indestructibility.[29] In the early stages of the myth Osiris is a fertility god, but the later myths show Osiris as more than the young fertility gods who were slain to ensure continuing fecundity. The stress laid upon Osiris was on his "everlasting" nature. He was not only a dying and rising god but one who does not die, who remains forever, indestructible; he is the very essence of life, the animating principle of life. "Dismemberment, sowing, and threshing are equivalent to destroying the personality and breaking down the living unit. . . . The principle opposed to this found embodiment in the mummification of the phallus . . . and the symbol of everlastingness is Osiris. Osiris as the dismembered god is the bringer of fertility, the young king who passes away and returns like the vegetation, but as the procreative mummy with the permanent phallus, he is everlasting and imperishable. Osiris, the fertile dead one, begets new life even though dead. In this mysterious symbol of the fertile dead resides a new insight: "the everlastingness and fruitfulness of the living spirit as opposed to the everlastingness and fruitfulness of nature."[30]

The earliest symbol for Osiris is the *djed* tree or pillar, which resembles a tree trunk whose stumps of branches project to either side at the top, resembling a rude cross. For the Egyptians, wood symbolized organic living nature, as opposed to the inorganic, dead duration of stone and the ephemeral life of vegetation. A central act in the ritual of Osiris is the "erection," the lifting of the *djed* pillar. This erection "symbolizes the resuscitation of Osiris, *i.e.*, the coming to life of the dead, and not the resurrection of a young vegetation god." On the following day, the New Year was ritually begun with the enthronement of the new king and celebrated as the anniversary of Horus, son of Osiris. The old conflict between the passing king and the new king has been overcome by a new psychic constellation in which the son has a positive relationship with the father. Neumann comments, "The restoration of Osiris is identical with his resurrection and transformation, which make him the king of the spirits, and his son king of the earth." Further, connecting this rite with the general practice and mythic understandings of totemism, Neumann says, "One of the basic phenomena of totemism and of all initiation rites is that the totem or ancestor is reincarnated in the initiate, finding in him a new dwelling place and at the same time constituting his higher self. This result can be traced all the way from the sonship of the Horus hero and its connection with the apotheosis of his father Osiris to the Christian Incarnation and the phenomenon of individuation in modern man."[31] The parallel with St. Paul's comment "no longer I, but Christ who lives in me" seems obvious.

In the matrilineal world of the planting peoples, death and resurrection occurred on the same earthly plane. Death meant the end of fertility, and resurrection meant the appearance of new vegetation. Both were still within the plane of Mother Nature. In Osiris, however, a change is observed.

> . . . resurrection means realizing his eternal and lasting essence, becoming a perfected soul, escaping from the flux of natural occurrence. The corollary of this is Horus' enthronement as the son of Osiris. As the son of Isis he would be no more than a fleeting god of vegetation. . . . Now, however, he is conjoined to the father, the everlasting and unchanging spiritual father who rules over the spirits. . . . When the ladder of Osiris is raised up in the coronation ceremonies, and the erection of the *djed* and elevation of the old king usher in the crowning of Horus, this means that his power is grounded in the higher father and no longer in the lower mother. [32]

This old Egyptian myth is clearly a Hero myth. It is the story of the human connection with God as the Divine Center and the human as the "son of God," whose divine sonship is latent from the beginning of life. This inherent divinity can be realized, however, only through the Hero journey in which the ego (Horus) is united with the Self (Osiris). In the course of further spiritual development, it was realized that resurrection to this eternal life was the proper destiny of every human. The human myth of each person as Hero is realized only when the individual ego identifies with the Self (Divine Center), in other words, "when it realizes that the support of heaven at the moment of death means nothing less than to be begotten by a god and born anew. Only in this paradoxical situation, when the personality experiences dying as a simultaneous act of self-reproduction, will the twofold man be reborn as the total man." [33]

The battle of the Hero in this final scene is to overcome to the fullest the alienation from the Mother (i.e., from those remaining aspects of the psyche that have not been hitherto accepted) and to rejoin Mother and Father in the center of the psyche, thus returning to paradise but with a major difference. The first paradise was the paradise of unconsciousness, before the Father God and his law enabled ego to come into its own. Now the joining of Mother and Father must mean joining with full ego-consciousness. This last reunion, as we can now understand it, must be carried out, or at least begun, by the voluntary sacrifice of ego *on the tree.* This voluntary sacrifice means a sacrifice not to some earthly institution, even a religious one, or to some earthly person, even a saint, but to the guiding energy of psyche itself, which means the androgynous rule of the Mother-Father God, who can now be seen to be one and with whom we are to become one.

The Hero's pain is the pain of total renunciation amidst an intense longing for life. The psychic energy that has flowed intensely into consciousness now falls into the depths of the psyche. In the final analysis, however, it is the work of the center of the psyche, the Self, which we may now identify as the Mother-Father center, or simply as the Divine Center, which brings about this last movement. The ego must decrease and the Divine Center increase in proportion, but at the same time the ego knows that it is one with the Father-Mother. Neumann wrote, "In the self the ego knows itself immortal, and in itself mortal. . . . By ceding its pretensions to uniqueness and its central position to the self, the ego, as its indirect representative, becomes 'king of this world,' just as the self is 'king of the spirit-world.'"[34] In this new identity with the Self the ego experiences resurrection, ascension, and eternal life.

As has been noted, this ultimate adventure of the Hero has, in myth, most commonly been told as the story of the sacred marriage. When all the preliminary ogres have been overcome, the Great Mother and Father Dragons slain and the princess freed, then comes the triumphant marriage with the Queen Goddess of the World. The marriage is the union of those principles of the psyche represented in Chinese philosophy as Yang and Yin, in myth by male and female, and in analytical psychology by conscious and unconscious. St. Augustine wrote of this union: "Like a bridegroom Christ went forth from his chamber, he went out with a presage of his nuptials into the field of the world. . . . He came to the marriage bed of the cross, and there, in mounting it, he consummated his marriage."[35] Only the Hero who has truly overcome the destructive powers of the unconscious, whether the powers be experienced internally or in projection, who has transcended the need for self-aggrandizement of ego, who truly stands for all humanity—only that Hero can join with the Divine Center. The Easter events thus symbolize in a supreme way the necessary conjunction of opposites, reaffirming and reestablishing the union of God and human. This one, who is united with the Father and the Mother, "is the whole man, [who] has been made whole by the integration of opposites. He has transcended the opposition of thou and I, of I and world, inside and out, friend and enemy, joy and sorrow. Devoid of good deeds, devoid of evil deeds, a knower of *brahman* [God], unto *brahman* he proceeds. . . . [He knows] himself to be 'light of the inexhaustible light.' "[36] Or as The Revelation to John reports Jesus' testimony, "I Jesus have sent my angel to you with this testimony for the churches. . . . The Spirit and the Bride say, 'Come.' And let him who is thirsty come, let him who desires take the water of life without price" (Rev. 22:16–17).

X

Summary and Conclusions

THROUGHOUT THIS BOOK I have tried to show that the essence of the human being is the psyche and that we must understand the psyche more fully if we are to understand our human knowing and doing. Psyche has produced a number of ways of being conscious, among them the cognitive/scientific and its polar opposite, the mythic/symbolic. I have tried to show that the mythic/symbolic is the older, more profound, natural language of psychic processes but that it has been largely disregarded in the modern world. Myth is the foundation of knowledge, meaning, and value. Myth is the organizing principle of every symbol system. When the myths fail or fall into the unconscious, life loses direction and meaning, as has happened in contemporary civilization. Myth is the story of the human psyche and its pilgrimage, its pitfalls and its goal. Myth is the principal tool in our construction of reality. Our perception is mythically ordered, not just a set of biological responses to external stimuli.

According to the scientific worldview of the nineteenth century, dominated by positivism, objective knowledge of the world was possible through scientific methods and mechanical equipment, which would eliminate subjective bias from observation. Nature would thus be known as it is, in itself, apart from errors of observation. Modern physics has rediscovered the role of the observer in data collection and analysis. The notion that reality exists apart from any observer and can be known per se, has been discredited. The observer partic-

ipates in the creation of reality by observing and does so through a
psychosocial process, a mythically ordered process.

The psyche is a language process, but its depths are ruled by
symbols. Symbols, unlike signs, have a character of mystery because they refer to somewhat or mostly unknown, perhaps unknowable, processes. Symbols have power in the psyche; they release,
direct, or channel psychic energy. Without a symbol, the process it
represents is unknowable, except as an emotion or a mood; the
symbol makes it present to ego-consciousness; that is, symbols are
the foundational elements of ego-consciousness. Symbols are not
intentionally created; they well up out of the mysterious depths of
psyche; they live and they die.

Jung's study of the symbolic processes of the psyche as represented in myth, dream, vision, and fantasy has disclosed a universal
psychic structure. He called the dynamic structuring elements *archetypes* and found the principal dynamics of the psyche to be the
ongoing relation between ego and the archetypes of the transpersonal psyche, particularly the central and all-pervasive archetype
called the *Self*. The Self is the senior partner in the psyche, and
ego's destiny is to be the agent of Self, but too often the developing
ego becomes alienated from its Divine Center. This state of inner
division is endemic and critical for modern civilization and corre-
lates with the modern myth of progress through applied human
ego-rationality. Ego is the center of consciousness and of will and
responsibility, but it does not control the whole psyche, or even its
own destiny. Ego perceives the external world and its internal
world in symbolic form, i.e., not directly, but coded in a mythic
code. Consciousness is mythic. Individually and collectively, we
live mythically. Mythology is a kind of catalogue of typical human
experiences, typical human ways of being. The culturally shared,
dominant myth is the basis for cultural reality, but the individual
has also a personal myth, which varies, more or less, from the cultural dominant. A person's relationship to the personal and shared
myth is best described as faith. The myth a person lives by is the
manifestation of the God or gods who have grasped the loyalty and
trust of that person's heart and mind.

The myth that has most powerfully grasped the hearts and

minds of Western civilization during the past few centuries has been termed rationalism, more specifically rationalistic material- ism. But the age of rationalism is drawing to a close as we discover the fallacies of its basic notions. Science, although rooted in the soil of rationalism, has in many ways pioneered the transcendence of ra- tionalism. Relativity, the quantum theory, the electromagnetic na- ture of the physical world, and the principle of indeterminacy have in various ways discredited the idea of positive knowledge of things as they are in themselves. The observer has been discovered to be an essential part of the creation of knowledge and reality. The emerging myth, or worldview, begins with the realization that we have no absolute way of stating the truth of the universe and that our scientific endeavors have not enlightened us about the mean- ing, purpose, or destiny of human existence (i.e., scientific endeav- ors have not created a value scheme for us to live by). Our vast knowledge of the world, when followed to its deepest levels, has made us far more aware of the amazing mystery of the universe. In- stead of being assured that we can indeed predict and control the future, we are now aware of our great ignorance, our limited power, and our own predilection for evil. We are rediscovering the critical importance of the gifts from or through the transpersonal psyche for the further creation of knowledge, hence an appreciation for dream, fantasy and intuition; an appreciation of the role of myth in construction of reality. The new knowledge can be self-critical of its mythic foundation because the new knowledge is aware of that foundation. No longer does the realm of spirit and imagination seem unreal or less real than the so-called material world; both realms are known only by inferences from consciousness, infer- ences shaped by mythic assumptions. The spiritual realm is the in- side, so to speak, of the material. Spirit is the realm of consciousness, meaning, purpose, value, choice, perception, and enjoyment. It is preeminently the realm of the human psyche, hence of symbol and myth. Religion and myth are indissolubly bound because myth is held by faith, and faith creates both God and idols for consciousness. (This statement does not imply that Eternal God is dependent on human faith for existence, only that faith is the way a particular myth of God or idol comes to exist and reign in consciousness; the Divine Center, God, is always living and dynamically active in the psyche of every person as well as on earth and "in heaven.") To be religious means to take something with ultimate seriousness because it ties us to our foundations.

Most of us are unaware of these distinctions; we simply live our lives somewhat unconsciously within the dominant myth/symbol system of the culture. However, once we realize that we do in fact "create" the world through the means of a myth/symbol system that is held in faith and that alternative myth/symbol systems exist, another question emerges: which alternative is best? How do we choose? I have advocated some criteria for selection: adequacy, appropriateness, internal and external consistency, and, most important, elegance. The universe, although seeming to prize diversity as well as harmony, or novelty as well as order, prizes neither category to the detriment of the other; rather, both properly function together to bring forth beauty.

The criterion of appropriateness is not met by most attempts to discuss psyche in scientific terms because the symbols used are not rich enough to do justice to the inner feelings of the experience being described. Yet, there is a natural, inherent symbol system of the psyche that does seem appropriate, a system embodied in dreams, vision, and myth. To speak in an organized fashion about that natural system requires another system, a metasymbol system. The latter is inherently a metapsychology because its object of study is the psyche's natural symbol system. According to Jung, such a metasystem is a way of viewing the archetypal images so as to reveal the dynamics of the psyche. Such a system also appears to meet the other criteria, including elegance, and it shows the psyche to be striving for beauty through its inherent polarities. Further, the study of the natural symbol system of the psyche discloses that it always seems to include symbols that refer to a transcendent center, or the Divine Center, which is also immanent in the individual psyche. Jung termed this center the Self, or the God archetype.

The proposed metasymbol system is simple, in accord with its mythic character, although in its exposition it is quite complex. The metamyth states that psyche is a process of symbols, a process that has an inherent pattern and direction, i.e., a goal or a destiny. Dynamically, the process of symbols is the story of the relationship between the center of consciousness, ego, and the center of the whole psyche, the Divine Center. Jung refused to identify the Self with God because that was a theological and metaphysical conclusion and he wished to confine his writings to psychology, but in this book the Self has been termed the Divine Center, the indwelling God of the New Testament, of which the human is the temple. Further, following the insight that God is the locus of the universe, or the medieval notion that God is a circle whose center is everywhere and whose circumference is nowhere, or Whitehead's notion that God is not the exception to but the chief exemplification of all metaphysical principles, we reach a natural connection, identifying the center of the individual psyche with the center of all things, the Divine Center of all.

A myth that is found worldwide, told in every language and among every people, is the Hero myth. This myth is the central story of psychic development in the human being. The dynamic of the story is the dynamic of the psyche itself, the relation between the ego and the Divine Center. Using the tool of the metamyth, the Hero myth can be read as the story of human development. Its versions vary somewhat, and some of them are tragic—the stories of failed Heroes. Nonetheless, a cross-cultural comparison discloses a surprising agreement about the complete Hero journey. Using the tool of the metamyth for the exposition of the Hero story in its ideal form may provide a check on the value of the metamyth, i.e., allow us to look at it in the light of the criteria I have suggested. Further, the exposition of a myth can shed light on the meaning of the metasystem itself by providing the richness missing in any scientific myth (hypothesis).

We find it difficult to understand the importance of viewing the essence of the human psyche as a process of symbols, in part because that process is nonmaterial, or spiritual, and we habitually operate on the rationalistic myth, which denies reality to the spiritual. We thus think rather automatically that there has to be something material of which the symbolic process is an effect. A second reason for our difficulty arises from our habit of knowing, of understanding of human perception positivistically, that is, as direct perception of reality per se, not as perception and knowing mediated through myth. I am convinced that psyche starts the knowing process by assigning certain of its own archetypal content to the encountered unknown, as one does in completing a Rorschach inkblot test. Through this assigning of archetypal content, usually called projection in psychology, an entity becomes visible and sensible to consciousness, even though the act of projection is unconscious. Ego is presented with the result, and we "experience as" though the unknown were an incarnation of the archetypal content. At least, some connection, some "hook," attracts and holds the projection; that is, the archetypal symbolism appropriately represents some aspect of that which it makes conscious. Ego tends to ignore the factor of *likeness* and experiences the result as true, honest cognition, as reality. Collective projection, i.e., the common projection of the same archetypal material, is usual among persons who share a common culture.

The content of the collective pattern of perception founded on projection, i.e., the "experiencing as if" the archetypal image were the unknown reality, is incorporated into, or is, the myth of the collective. Once established, the pattern is then taught by socialization as the proper way to "construct" reality. The content always includes primary notions about nature, the human, and God (even if the idea be atheism). The more unconscious we are of this process and its content, the fewer choices we have in life. Apart from a conscious use of symbol, psychic energy is released unconsciously to the stimulus; we do no real choosing at all. We usually note those who stand out from the collective mass (e.g., psychotics, neurotics, and children) as being at the mercy of their unconscious, but we fail to note that the collective mass is equally dominated by an unconscious phenomenon that Levy-Bruhl termed *participation mystique* and that David Riesman termed *other-directed behavior*. Transcending mere collective behavior has been and is a primary goal in psychic development. This goal is not invented by ego but is archetypally founded; it is inherent in the symbol system of the psyche, over which the Divine Center presides. The development of the psyche is, in general, an archetypally founded process, led by the Self. But the urge to development along the Hero pattern is not inevitable, unless we allow for more or less instant development during the process of dying. Some people, perhaps the majority of the human race, seem to go through life quite unconsciously.

The conscious symbol has been the means by which the control of instincts and the building of the spiritual life has proceeded. Organized religions offer a symbol system that functions as a counterpole to primitive, instinctual nature. If we are to develop, however, each previous set of collective beliefs must be transcended. Hence, any advance in spirituality begins with an individual who breaks through at least some of the dominant collective beliefs. This process can occur whenever an individual consciousness is offered, from the transpersonal psyche, a new archetypal image. The symbols created in the psyche are always grounded in archetypal roots, but their overt form is often shaped by objects in the environment, e.g., rivers, trees, mother, father, the ocean, mountains, sun, moon, animals. These objects seem to be self-selected or attracted by the archetype itself, not consciously chosen by ego. As such, the objects, whether positive or negative, display a numinous, mysterious, luring quality.

The archetype par excellence of development and renewal is the Hero. The Hero archetype stimulates and guides, lures and inspires the development of human consciousness. Because the human psyche is the source of all cultural and religious phenomena, the secret to understanding them is also locked into the Hero pattern. Other archetypes are at work as well, but in the main can be regarded in how they articulate with the dynamics of the Hero. Consider again Neumann's comment:

> Thus the hero is the archetypal forerunner of mankind in general. His fate is the pattern in accordance with which the masses of humanity must live, and always have lived, however haltingly and distantly; and however short of the ideal man they have fallen, the stages of the hero myth have become constituent elements in the personal development of every individual.[1]

The story of particular Heroes is told always in mythic form, i.e., woven in archetypal imagery; the historical person's story is "experienced as" if it conformed to the archetype and is thus told as an archetypal tale, a myth. The Hero myth is a central paradigm in every culture. Campbell's studies have disclosed that these stories have a universal pattern into which individual variations have been woven; the universal is the outline of the archetype. The Hero story that has been most influential in Western civilization is the story of Jesus, as told in the New Testament and extrapolated in dogma. The Hero is the archetypal forerunner of humanity in general, but the form that the story has taken in Western thought and literature is exemplified in the story of Jesus.

The Jesus-Hero story has been discussed in four steps: birth, departure and initiation, battle with the dragon, and sacred marriage (including death and resurrection). I maintain that these steps are stages of psychic development, the pilgrimage of the soul, and that they center on the development of ego-consciousness and its destiny as the ego relates to (1) the Divine Center, (2) other persons, especially significant others, e.g., mother and father, (3) the collective and its mores, (4) itself, (5) the various archetypal figures, and (6) the nonhuman environment. Rather than recapping the Jesus story here, I will review the story as the pilgrimage of ego-consciousness. The difficulty in such a process was recognized by Neumann:

> Our contention that the development of ego consciousness is depicted in myth is, however, complicated by the fact that while we take the myth literally and describe the experiences of the youthful lover, for example, "as if" he were a living figure, we must simultaneously interpret him as the symbolical representative of a definite ego stage in man's development.[2]

The Hero is born of the virgin mother. The virgin proper is the transpersonal psyche (Jung's collective unconscious), the realm of the archetypes. At the time of biological birth, ego is only a germ of potential, an archetype, contained in the transpersonal psyche. For centuries, lost in the millennia of time, this potential slept in the Mother unconscious. Then, at some point known only to divine reckoning, the procreative masculine, which is also at work in the dark feminine world of the unconscious, became active and ego began to be born in psyche. (Note: *masculine* and *feminine* are used here as before, not to refer to human sexual distinctions but to the symbolic patterns presented in myth and dream.) The Father Spirit is the procreative aspect of the Divine Center, the God archetype of the psyche. In the oceanic stage, before the development of consciousness, there is no symbolic process because *symbol* is used here to mean a process of consciousness. Consciousness arises together with symbols. Only when symbols exist are perception and choice possible. The activation of the Father Spirit (the Great Father) fecundates the Great Mother unconscious and results in the birth of symbols and of ego-consciousness. The Great Father is the creative principle of the psyche. "Not only does this principle direct the metabolism of the life forces, not only does it balance and compensate, it also leads to the development of new unities, giving rise to new organs and systems of organs, and trying its hand at creative experiments."[3] The Divine Center calls into being in the primordial, undifferentiated psyche a subsidiary center of consciousness, a center that is occupied by ego. It is the role, the intended destiny, of ego to represent the interest of the total person against particular demands that come from within or without. Symbolically, the ego is related to the Divine Center as a child, in the myth of Jesus, as a son. Ego's destiny is to be a center of consciousness on behalf of the Divine Center. Consciousness is typically symbolized by light, and the Hero is typically connected with the sun god, hence born on the sun's birthday, the midwinter solstice.

Ego is not born into a world free of conflict. From the onset, ego-consciousness is beset by two enemies: the inertia of instinct, which would keep the ego asleep, and the structures of culture, which would fit the ego to a procrustean bed of conformity, i.e., the Terrible Mother and the Terrible Father. Humans lived in the sleepy realm of instinct for untold millennia, and that realm reclaims consciousness every night in sleep; after its birth, ego must struggle against these inertial and cultural forces. Only through victory in this lengthy battle does ego prepare itself to be a worthy child of the Divine Center, a child that can be trusted with higher

powers. Intentional symbols, the gift of the Father Spirit, mark the
crossover from instinct to intention, from automatism to responsibility. "The symbolic expression of instinctive forces drags them
out into the open; it differentiates them and delineates them."[4] The
coming of ego is a "new thing" wrought by the Divine Center in
the unchanging world of the eternal return, the instinctual psyche.
The continuing nurturance of this child is the task of religion and
culture, but each has its inertial side—the Terrible Father, who
fears any new development.

Gradually, the developing ego comes to an awareness of individual identity. This sense of individuality is an important development in the history of consciousness. For literally thousands of
years humanity lived with only a collective sense of identity. Indeed, not until the modern period of history have most persons
possessed a sense of personal, individual identity. Before them,
humans were collective-minded, living almost identical lives of
participation mystique. The sense of personal identity is crystal-
lized by some event, external or internal, that calls us to our desti-
nies. The calling itself may be of small importance as an event, but
its effect is to start a process of death and rebirth within the psyche;
it marks the transition from collective to individual being. Not
everyone heeds this calling; many indeed prefer the easier, more
comfortable choices that the collective way offers. The consciousness of being called is an awareness of uniqueness, of having a special destiny. In the story of the Hero Jesus, this event is the story of
his encounter and baptism by John the Baptist. In and through this
event, Jesus discovers his messianic vocation. Baptism signifies a
return to the Great Mother unconscious, fountain of all being, from
which one is reborn as a new being, consciously dedicated to the
purpose of the calling. The calling itself we may see as the work of
the Divine Center. For, like the birth of ego and the initiation to
follow, the calling is instigated by the Father Spirit. When the ego
heeds the lure of the Father Spirit, ego and consciousness become
the bearers of psychic development.

With the onset of a conscious identity, the conscious personality,
the ego, now assumes an attitude and a relationship toward the
realm of the unconscious or at least toward its promptings. Jung dis-

covered that this relationship is personified by an inner figure of the psyche, which has for men a feminine character and for women a masculine character—the anima and the animus. This figure mediates the relationship of ego-consciousness to the transpersonal psyche and to the Divine Center. At this point of development, this inner figure confronts the Ego-Hero with a trial, a testing, that must be successfully passed before further psychic development can occur. For Jesus, this trial, the initiation proper of the Hero, is his forty-day testing in the wilderness at the hands of Satan. This initiation has a distinct resemblance to the vision quest of the shaman and perhaps is connected with the precipitating vision that seems to have formed the onset of the prophet's vocation in ancient Israel.

Satan has been connected with the dark, unconscious side of ego, the Shadow. Mythic material often depicts the Shadow as the dark brother of the Hero, such as Cain to Abel or Set to Osiris. Jung viewed the Shadow as the necessary opponent who participates in the psychic struggle for development. In mortal conflict with this figure, ego must struggle to defend its own values and destiny against its inner temptation to give in to various drives for pleasure or power. Its own values are those given in the gift of calling and insight from the Father Spirit, the deepest voice of conscience (not social mores). The realization of this inner conflict, the encounter with one's own Shadow potentials, has a very humbling effect. This humility makes ego aware that evil is not just something that belongs to others. The dark potentials of humanity belong to every ego in some degree. If ego does not discover this inner darkness as its own and learn to cope with it, ego will likely succumb to thinking of itself as destined to personal glory or power and thus become possessed of overweening pride, hubris, inflation. A great many human political, industrial, religious, and other social leaders seem to have fallen victim to this peril. But the ego that becomes aware of its own limits and dependence in relationship to the transcendent Self and the transpersonal psyche as a whole, receives new and mysterious support from these forces. Further, the Shadow is not composed of only negative forces but contains many positive aspects of consciousness that have been rejected and need to be reclaimed. Although the overall experience is a humbling

one, a chastening one, it also is often experienced as a new sense of
personal destiny and a confidence about one's life, accompanied by
increased creative capacity and abilities that seem miraculous in
comparison with ordinary capacity and abilities. For the ego that
accepts its calling, life is now to be lived under the aegis of the
destiny revealed in the calling and with the capabilities and wisdom
discovered in the initiatory testing. Life has direction and purpose,
encompassing the assurance of a personal myth of destiny and a
firm filial relationship with the Father Spirit. From this point the
highest commitment of the Ego-Hero is relationship to the Divine
Center and attunement to the inner voice or vision through which
the Divine Center communicates. The communication may be experienced in dreams, visions, imagination, or fantasy, or simply as a
dim presentiment of direction in the push and pull of daily life.
This pattern, the essence of being religious, must be lived out in
the world, at least for the most part, although some people are
clearly called to be reclusives and contemplatives.

Calling and initiation require death and rebirth, which are symbolized in primitive groups in dramatic and powerful rites and are
symbolized in the tradition of Christianity in conversion and baptism. But the events proper are inward events, not caused by rites,
although administered appropriately and at the right time, a rite
may precipitate transformation. Until the calling, one lives in the
bosom of the family and enjoys a given identity. Rules for behavior
and goals for life are set from the outside, by community or parents. The new identity and purpose from the Divine Center drive
one into the unknown (the wilderness, in the New Testament). One
can go, like the prodigal son of Jesus' parable, claiming inheritance
and freedom only to squander them on indulging the lusts of flesh
and spirit (one then usually ends up in the pigsties of life, resulting
in a renewed demand for insight). The fundamental questions are
those of personal identity and relationship: Who are you to be
when you're on your own, not under the scrutiny of family or the
collective? What do *you* value (not just what do the mores say)? In
our culture these life experiences are usually played out between
our high school years and age thirty-five. This passage is, however,
a very difficult one and when the school system is dominated by an

essentially cerebral ethos, a tragic rate of failure in making this transition is to be expected. Prominent in this essentially cerebral ethos is the rationalistic myth, with its distrust of dream, vision, and spirit.

The essentially inner conflict between the lure of the spiritual principle (represented in anima or animus) and the introjected forces of socialization (backed by the collective) soon breaks into a more open conflict as one tries to live according to the personal inner vision. The Hero now meets the outer dragonlike forces, which would mold the individual to fit and serve society's status quo first and which allows only such personal identity as does not seem likely to conflict. In the symbolic stories of myth these collective forces are often depicted as great fire-breathing dragons who must be defeated if one is to win the fair young maiden, one's soul. Such stories often include a wicked king or an old, weak king who has no queen. The tyrant king is an ego gone wrong, following its own lust for pleasure, power, or glory rather than serving the Divine Center. The old, weak king is sterile, as symbolized by the lack of a queen, and thus can have no more children, no renewal, no new life. The story of the barren fig tree in the New Testament is the equivalent of the barren king. When collective consciousness stiffens into doctrines, rules, or laws, its connection with its creative ground, the transpersonal psyche, is lost; it has lost Eros, and further spiritual development is blocked.

The Ego-Hero, which is connected to the creative ground, will inevitably come into conflict with these negative forces of culture. After the renewal of initiation the Hero is remarkably different because he possesses an inner authority. The Ego-Hero thus no longer lives strictly according to the collective "but by every word that proceeds from the mouth of God" (Matt. 4:4). This inner authority and insight are not to be kept selfishly but to be shared; thus, the ego is called to be an agent to enlighten and free others. This call means a battle against the "fathers," who symbolize the world of collective values ruled by the aged or tyrant king. The Ego-Hero must oppose the absolute authority the fathers claim for themselves and their law, their canon of values. The task is to "awaken the sleeping images of the future which can and must come forth from the night, in order to give the world a new and better face."[5] Thus, the Hero is most likely to be perceived as a breaker of the law, an enemy of law and order, a disturber of the status quo, a cultural rebel, and an immoral person. Psychologically, it is not rivalry for the mother that is involved in the "killing of the father" but the overcoming of the oppressive authority of the "conscience," the introjected value system of the patriarchy, the authoritarian side of the Father archetype, i.e., the spiritual Terrible Father.

For us today, the Terrible Father is found not so much in the collective forces of religion as in the dogmas of rationalism and the view of science it spawned. Presented to us as scientific fact, the true vision of reality, this myth has alienated ego-consciousness from its creative ground in the transpersonal psyche. A fascinating development has, however, been brought about by the physicists who have pushed beyond collective wisdom. As noted in Zukav's quote in the Introduction, the new physicist is aware that humanity has put far too much faith in science to tell us about the nature and purpose of life and failed to recognize the limits of scientific knowledge. The final word from Zukav was to point out that the scientists, after three centuries of work, are saying that "the key to understanding the universe is you."[6] Only as we come to know ourselves, our processes of perception, our mythic way of constructing reality, can we become more adequately related to the processes of the universe that surround us. It is the "ossified structures of perception [which] are the prisons in which we unknowingly become prisoners."[7] The cure for the split psyche is not a *return* to traditional values and beliefs but the faithful following of the lure of the contrasexual aspect of psyche into the depths. When the Ego-Hero overcomes the Terrible Father dragon, the inner princess is freed and will lead the ego, as Beatrice led Dante, to the depths and the heights of psyche.

The first encounter with this contrasexual aspect of psyche is usually through projection onto a person with whom we fall in love. "It is the recognition of 'our native country' through love of another. We glimpse his or her eternal identity and so also our own, and we know in that moment that we have the freedom of that country forever."[8] Too often, we fail to glimpse the loved one's eternal identity; instead, we fall, like the prodigal, into the love of the sensual, and soon even that is lost in everydayness. But if we catch that glimpse and follow it, the inner, eternal nature comes into view; if we observe that nature clearly, it becomes apparent that she or he gazes forever at the Divine Center. This is the beginning of the final reorientation and transformation of ego. This discovery and realization, in mythological terms, bring us to the Sacred Marriage.

Just as the preparation for the battle with the Terrible Father dragon required the purging days in the wilderness, so the preparation for the sacred marriage requires certain internal work; in this case the careful observation and following of the inward way of dream, vision, and imagination. The person who successfully traverses the first dragon battle, overcoming the lures and temptations of the unconscious and the tie to Mother and childhood, confronts the anima or animus in an external beloved by way of projection. This projection gives the psyche an outward gradient. The Hero myth of Jesus treats this aspect of his life only minimally. Yet there is evidence that he was close to several women—the sisters Mary and Martha, and Mary Magdalene—and he was publicly criticized for his friendship with ladies of ill repute. From the depth of his feelings and emotions, we can infer that he successfully withdrew his anima projections and incorporated his own inner feminine aspect that had previously been projected onto one or more of these women.

Beyond the second dragon battle against the Terrible Father, embodied in the collective, the anima or animus is again activated, but now as a lure and guide into the depths of psyche to the Divine Center. This activation results in a decreased interest in the outer world and the formation of a gradient toward the center. In the previous period the main work has been the building of ego through human relationships, personal achievements, power, or creative work. In this new period, the second half of life, the work comprises the assimilation of transpersonal and suprapersonal contents, and the center of life gradually shifts from the ego to the Divine Center. This shift means that the ego must make a heroic journey to the underworld of psyche. One may not go this way without dedication and perseverance, nor may one go in an emotional romantic plunge or in a dust-dry academic quest. This quest is like the pursuit of the Holy Grail. Any way other than the way of devotion leads to the loss of the guide and likely to inundation by the forces of the negative unconscious. It further requires the final purgation of ego-centeredness from one's life.

The Hero represents the destiny of the ego. As "Son of God" this archetype is peculiarly related to the Divine Center and thus to the Ultimate God. The Sacred Marriage represents the union of the conscious and the unconscious aspects of psyche; the full integration of psyche proceeds beyond this union in the uniting with the Divine Center. Such a process means a significant shift for ego, for it no longer will regard itself as the center except in a strictly secondary sense. The Apostle Paul was sensing this shift when he wrote, "no longer I, but Christ in me." The king (ego) must die and be reborn. The process is twofold, and the motifs are intertwined: the freeing of the captive and the Hero's union with her, and the death and resurrection-ascension of the Hero. The first motif points to the wholeness and healing of the split psyche and the second to the final destiny of the human—union with the Divine Center. As long as ego is alienated from its foundation in the transpersonal, locked in the world of consciousness, it is like the barren fig tree, unable to produce its fruit in due season. The only way beyond this barrenness requires a self-sacrifice of ego to the mysterious transpersonal depths of psyche. This sacrifice often occurs gradually, perhaps over years, even though its onset may be marked by a dramatic event or decision. Further, the sacrifice is not merely for the sake of personal spiritual gain, for that might well be only further ego-aggrandizement. As T. S. Eliot wrote, "The last temptation then is the greatest treason: To do the right deed for the wrong reason" (*Murder in the Cathedral*, pt. 1). The sacrifice comes at the prompting of the Divine Center; ego exclaims, "Thy will be done!" and the outcome redounds to the benefit of all—"This is my body broken for you." Yet the sacrifice is also an act, a decision of ego, a voluntary sacrifice.

This final sacrifice comes at a point of great tension, by which ego is torn between contradictory aspects of life. The cross is peculiarly appropriate to symbolize this tension and tearing. We do not know the precise tension that gripped Jesus, yet his night of agony in Gethsemane certainly attests to the power of the struggle in which he was engaged. Out of that struggle was born the conviction and courage to walk openly into the carefully laid trap and let the authorities have their way, even though that path led to crucifixion. Perhaps the way of Judas the zealot and the way of the mystic of the transfiguration suggest the crossed ways that lured Jesus—the way of the political activist versus the way of the religious contemplative. Out of this struggle and agony came an inner resolution forever symbolized by the words "Thy will be done."

This final sacrifice of the Ego-Hero is not to some earthly institution or person but to the guiding energy of the psyche itself. Ego yields fully and finally to the kingship of the Divine Center, thereby becoming united with the center of all. In this new identity with God, the Hero experiences resurrection and ascension, becomes a participant in the indestructibility of the Divine Life. The symbolism of crucifixion means the surrender of the whole of consciousness to the Divine Center, which now becomes the center of the whole personality. As the first Adam, by his relationship to a tree, brought death, so this second Adam, through death on the tree, brings eternal life. The wholeness that comes into being through ego's final union with the Divine is everlasting wholeness. Finitude is transcended, and the ego is now a recipient of a light as unfailing as that of the sun. Resurrection is the realization of that which "no eye has seen, nor ear heard, nor the heart of man conceived, what God has prepared for those who love him" (1 Cor. 2:9). This life transcends death, or perhaps better, this transcendent life finds death to be a doorway to greater life, to fulfillment.

> Then I saw a new heaven and a new earth; for the first heaven and the first earth had passed away, and the sea was no more. And I saw the holy city, new Jerusalem, coming down out of heaven from God, prepared as a bride adorned for her husband; and I heard a loud voice from the throne saying, "Behold, the dwelling of God is with men. . . . and death shall be no more, . . . for the former things have passed away." (Rev. 21:1–4)

Early in this book I enunciated the thesis that human beings live by myth; later, I expounded the Hero myth that has been central to Western civilization for some two thousand years. I have argued that because we now know we live by myth, we can and must raise a new question, "Which myth shall be dominant, and why?" Several criteria for choosing among myths have been advanced—adequacy, appropriateness, internal and external consistency, and, most important, elegance. Further, I described a metamyth that, as a transformation key, would unlock the meaning of the natural symbols of psyche and then used that metamyth to interpret the Hero myth.

The question to be faced now is, does it all hang together? Does the metamyth significantly clarify the Hero myth? Does it enable us to "make sense" out of our own experience of life, i.e., is life as the myth says it is? Does the teaching of this myth enable us to face the creative force we feel at work within us and to unfold the meaning that lies concealed in the depths of our existence? These questions are not so much theoretical or academic as they are existential; hence, they cannot be answered by mere words or logic. Only those who try to live by a myth can know its power for good or ill. Does a hidden current move within you, continuously calling life forward? Luring, cajoling, and even torturing you to surmount every pleasant status quo? Insisting that all aspects of life have meaning and place and cannot be ignored? Finally driving ego to the brink of madness, at which point ego surrenders its claim to autonomy in the psyche? If you and others recognize these sensations, the mythic way can make some sense of otherwise merely painful and perilous symptoms. The Hero myth can release and channel blocked psychic energy and free it to create new life, for the myth calls each ego to the pilgrimage of the soul, to its own destiny as ego yields its sovereignty and says, "Thy will be done."

Although the basis for any decision regarding the validity of these theses is existential rather than academic, nonetheless, some rational and empirical evidence may be cited. Jung found empirical evidence a great help in the support of his emerging ideas and discoveries about the psyche, particularly the discovery that *The Secret of the Golden Flower*, an ancient Chinese treatise sent him by

Richard Wilhelm, contained a schema of development and notions of the circumambulation of a transcendent center much like those Jung himself had discovered. So it is feasible to look for other confirmation of the pattern of development I propose. Note first the opening sentence of Ignatius Loyola's *Foundation*, "The human was created to praise, do reverence to, and serve God our Lord, and thereby to save the soul." Jung paraphrased and explained as follows: "Man's consciousness was created to the end that it may (1) recognize (*laudet*) its descent from a higher unity (*Deum*); (2) pay due and careful regard to this source (*reverentiam exhibeat*); (3) execute its commands intelligently and responsibly (*serviat*); and (4) thereby afford the psyche as a whole the optimum degree of life and development (*salvet animam suam*)."[9] These words, clearly a statement of the Christian life, generally support the view I advocated as the meaning of the Hero myth.

Second, note Aldous Huxley's summary of the insights of the world's higher religions, their Highest Common Factor, or Perennial Philosophy, as he calls it. The four fundamental doctrines are as follows:

> First: the phenomenal world of matter and of individualized consciousness—the world of things and animals and men and even gods—is the manifestation of a Divine Ground within which all partial realities have their being, and apart from which they would be nonexistent.
>
> Second: human beings are capable not merely of knowing *about* the Divine Ground by inference; they can also realize its existence by a direct intuition, superior to discursive reasoning. This immediate knowledge unites the knower with that which is known.
>
> Third: man possesses a double nature, a phenomenal ego and an eternal Self, which is the inner man, the spirit, the spark of divinity within the soul. It is possible for a man, if he so desires, to identify himself with the Spirit and therefore with the Divine Ground, which is of the same or like nature with the spirit.
>
> Fourth: man's life on earth has only one end and purpose: to identify himself with his eternal Self and so to come to unitive knowledge of the Divine Ground.[10]

The point of the Hero myth as I have analyzed it and the point as seen by Ignatius and Huxley appear to be the same: the purpose and goal of human history is the unfolding of human consciousness to its acme, which is the realization of oneness with the Ultimate Whole of the universe—that which religions call God. The Hero myth of Jesus is the story of one who lived out that process to its goal and thereby was a prototype for humanity. As such, he was indeed "fully man and fully God." Those who follow the Hero way to its culmination will also realize their oneness with the Ultimate Whole, not as a principle, a fact to be believed, but as an existential experience, a person's true identity.

Before one learns to take seriously the guidance of the inner spirit (living in the modern world as an ego-centered consciousness cut off from the foundations in the transpersonal), life is experienced as a part, a fragment, and one is a separate individual, cut off from the whole. Albert Einstein observed:

> A human being is a part of the whole, called by us "Universe"; a part limited in time and space. He experiences himself, his thoughts and feelings as something separated from the rest—a kind of optical delusion of his consciousness. This delusion is a kind of prison for us, restricting us to our personal desires and to affection for a few persons nearest us. Our task must be to free ourselves from this prison.[11]

Indeed, this individualized, ego-centered identity is a prison, the endemic prison of the modern human. But our imprisonment need not be terminal; it is not the fate or the destiny of the human being. Our commitment to the rationalistic myth has built the prison. The death of that myth is upon us, and the way is now open to allow us to transcend it. Sensitive persons have long realized that a way other than the dull, reductive logic of positivism is open to us. Again, as Einstein observed:

> The most beautiful emotion we can experience is the mystical. It is the sower of all true art and science. He to whom this emotion is a stranger . . . is as good as dead. To know that what is impenetrable to us really exists, manifesting itself as the highest wisdom and the most radiant beauty, which our dull faculties can comprehend only in their most primitive forms—this knowledge, this feeling, is at the center of true religiousness. In this sense, and in this sense only I belong to the ranks of devoutly religious men.[12]

Unveiling the inner structure of the Hero myth of Jesus allows us to discover Christianity's link not only with other world religions but with the perennial philosophy. Ken Wilber attributes the philosophy to "the great majority of the truly gifted theologians, . . . sages, and even scientists of various times."[13] A view of life advocated by Christian mystics, it forms the core of Hinduism, Buddhism, Taoism, Sufism, and Jewish mysticism. Seeing Jesus through the Gospels as the incarnation of the archetype of the Hero and knowing that archetype as the power behind ego-consciousness and its destiny show the necessary commonality of all these profound insights into the human. For we are, one and all, under the sway of this archetype, called to our destiny of realizing our oneness with the Ultimate Whole. For Western civilization the power of the Hero myth of Jesus has led and lured ego-consciousness to that stage of development during which the rationalistic myth, claiming to be the only truth, displaced the Hero myth. The collapse of the myth of rationalism will now allow us the choice of a better way, a way beyond the merely rational ego. The way illuminated by the myth of Jesus as Hero coincides with a resurgence of mystical insight and practice, supported by the influx of Eastern religions and their meditative practices. It is a way beyond ego-centered consciousness to a consciousness oriented to the Divine Center, a realization of oneness with the Ultimate Whole.

The modern way of consciousness centered on ego and experiencing-creating the world in the mode of rationalism is an inherently alienated way of life. Ego is thereby cut off from its ground and goal in the transpersonal psyche and from its destiny, which is union with the Divine Center. In the rationalistic mode, ego blows itself up as the center and very purpose of consciousness, indeed, the very purpose of the universe. Then all experiences are evaluated by their effect upon ego. This ego-centered mode, which lies at the heart of contemporary existence, results in life-experience that feels incomplete and insecure, purposeless and meaningless. Existentialists have extensively described this tragic emptiness in prose, drama, and verse. The fundamental and inescapable feeling (whether stated optimistically or pessimistically) that something in life is wrong or missing is the prompting of the Divine Center, which urges us to get on with the spiritual journey, the Hero journey, the ascent through the levels of consciousness to transcendence.

A growing consensus among many points of view is that life is essentially some kind of journey. In scientific terms this discernment is usually reported in ideas of evolution or development, change from a lesser to a greater, or lower to higher, less integrated to more integrated state. Political and social thought uses much the same vocabulary. In the religious realm the terms are pilgrimage, journey, ascent, and sanctification or growth in grace. History and biography borrow from, illustrate, and sometimes inspire the religious, political, social, and personal realms of life. So also do novels, plays, and poetry. The point is simply that wherever we turn, the human life is viewed as movement, process toward destiny. Throughout this book, I have argued that this process is essential to the human and that our modern way of consciousness has profoundly alienated us from our proper destiny. Thus do we suffer from the pangs of alienation and the lack of movement toward our destiny, both collectively and individually: this condition is the peculiar modern malaise. Our problem is not political, social, or economic in origin, but spiritual, religious. Our myth has fixated consciousness in one form, a very limiting form that excludes what earlier humans have recognized as the goal toward which life strives.

Our modern myth may be appropriately termed a *closed* myth. As I have explained, myth participates in the human construction of reality in a critical and necessary way; so much so that we must say, "no myth, no ego-consciousness," hence, no conscious reality (i.e., if there is no mythic construction of a world, one lives, like the neonate, without ego-consciousness). Closed myth leads to the construction of closed reality. Such reality is created, perceived as bounded by space-time, three-dimensional space, unidirectional time, inescapable cause and effect, a universe of chance, not teleological, hence not meaningful. Life is reduced to mechanism without purpose or destiny. The possibilities of such a way of creating-perceiving reality are illustrated by George Orwell's political vision in *1984* or B. F. Skinner's misguided vision of psychological utopia,

Beyond Freedom and Dignity. Much more influential incarnations of this myth have sprung out of Marx's enunciations of it in political-economic terms and Freud's enunciation in psychological terms.

Closed myth creates a world dominated by entropy; death is the ultimate outcome. Closed myth precludes the proper development of consciousness, its movement toward the Divine Center; it frustrates and blocks the urges and the lures from the Divine Center and reduces its inspiring symbols of dream and vision to mere signs or symptoms of biological mechanism. It leads us to view reality as divided by boundaries that separate opposites, which are then discerned as a pair of possibilities— one desirable, the other undesirable, positive and negative. Dividing the world into "common and preferred" displays the fall of Adam and Eve in eating from the fruit of the tree of the knowledge of good and evil.

> Perhaps we can begin to understand why life, when viewed as a world of separate opposites, is so totally frustrating, and why progress has actually become not a growth but a cancer. In trying to separate the opposites and cling to those we judge positive, such as pleasure without pain, life without death, good without evil, we are really striving after phantoms without the least reality. Might as well strive for a world of crests and no troughs, buyers and no sellers, lefts and no rights, ins and no outs. Thus, as Wittgenstein pointed out, because our goals are not lofty but illusory, our problems are not difficult but nonsensical.[14]

Open myth, by contrast, mediates the energies of life from the Divine Center, energies that do not end in death by entropy or biology but lead to eternal life. Open myth encourages and incarnates the development of consciousness in its movement toward the Divine Center. Open myth incorporates as its growing edge the new symbols and myths that emerge as consciousness grows toward apotheosis. Divisive boundaries are seen as barriers to be transcended until one finally knows unitive consciousness, oneness with all that is. Through open myth, consciousness is led to the transcendence of the fall at the tree of good and evil through the crucifixion of ego. The primary characteristic of open myth is that it continually points beyond itself to its source, the transcendent Divine Center. It turns us from speculation and reasoning about reality to that which creates and transcends every perceived reality and every expression of reality. Open myth is self-critical, professing its own inadequacy vis à vis the ultimacy of the Divine Center. The Jesus-Hero story directs consciousness to the transcendence of the opposites it has created until consciousness is finally at one with the Ultimate Reality, which is the unity of all opposites. Closed myth, the creation of opposites through boundaries, is the sin of Adam and Eve, the sin in which we all participate. As consciousness divides the world into good and evil, it eats of the forbidden, but necessary, fruit.

Ego-centered consciousness necessarily involved a "fall" into anxiety, into an experience that in religious terms is defined as being lost in sin, in effect dead in sin, cut off from life. In anxiety, ego seeks ways to deny its death experience, both present and future. It does this by denial, repression, and dilution. The primary repression in which ego engages is its repression of the consciousness of death.[15] Using the Hindu concept of Atman, which means ultimate, undivided reality and recognition of it as the proper identity-center of the human, Ken Wilber describes the human problem as our eternal preoccupation with the Atman Project. This project is a substitute for the realization, the consciousness of being at one with Atman, of Atman consciousness. Atman is ultimate wholeness, eternal and timeless, all-encompassing: "an integral Whole, outside of which nothing exists, it embraces all space and time, and is itself therefore spaceless and timeless, infinite and eternal."[16] Ego-centered consciousness of any form alienates us from Atman and leaves us with an anxious sense of emptiness, incompleteness, unconsciously longing for Atman.

> For every individual constantly intuits that his prior Nature is infinite and eternal, All and Whole—he is possessed, that is, with a true Atman intuition. But, at the same time, he is terrified of real transcendence, because transcendence entails the "death" of his isolated and separate-self sense. Because he won't let go of and die to his separate self, he cannot find true and real transcendence, he cannot find that larger fulfillment in integral Wholeness. Holding on to himself, he shuts out Atman; grasping only his own ego, he denies the rest of the All.[17]

Prizing the isolated ego as his or her *real* self, a person refuses the death of this separate-self identity and thus "goes about seeking transcendence in ways that *actually prevent* it and force symbolic substitutes."[18] Ego is substituted for Atman, and this false substitution is then defended by the ego's death avoidance and attempts to compensate for its lack of wholeness. Wilber discerns two main drives in the Atman Project: one, the perpetuation of ego's own existence, which he terms *Eros*; the other, the avoidance of all that threatens ego's dissolution, which he terms *Thanatos*. Ego carries out this twofold project primarily through culture, the world of objective substitute gratifications for Atman. Culture then provides Eros needs (life, power, stability, pleasure, mana), and protects against Thanatos (death, diminution, taboo).[19] Wilber's Atman Project is the creation and dwelling within a closed myth, a limited consciousness that has fixed its own boundaries and called them absolute.

The adventure of the Hero, to which all of us are called, is one of transcending the successive boundaries that establish consciousness in a limited form until the final state, which is the coincidence of opposites. To accomplish the pivotal feats, we must (1) go beyond unconsciousness to ego-consciousness; (2) battle past the childhood dragons of instinctual hungers to a mature, rational ego-consciousness; (3) go beyond the acculturated ego-consciousness to a consciousness devoted to the Divine Center; and (4) go beyond the separation from the Divine Center to unity, the unified consciousness of Christ or Buddha or Lao Tse. This ascension of consciousness is the successive transcendence of boundaries.

Because Ultimate Reality (God) has no boundaries, a boundary (and every state of consciousness below the level of uniting consciousness is founded in a myth of boundaries) that is presumed to be absolute (i.e., of divine authority) is always idolatrous. Closed myths are inherently idolatrous. A closed myth can be opened simply by acknowledging that it is provisional and denying that it has absolute character. But if one's consciousness, whether acknowledged or naïve, is based on the absoluteness of the particular myth, denying its absolute character is tantamount to death for that level of consciousness and transformation to a new state. So we reconnect with the Hero myth, from which we learned that each transformation is death and rebirth. Closed myth constitutes the wheel of finitude, the plights of Ixion and Prometheus and Adam. Closed myth is a description of a universe that has absolute boundaries. We humans, including theologians and scientists, become so enamored of our myths that we forget that the boundaries thus created are conventional. Wilber wrote that in the world of physics "they developed laws governing separate things, only to discover that separate things don't exist."[20]

The world is created by consciousness through myth. This world, however, is the created world, *our* creation. Beneath that or, better, beyond it, is Ultimate Reality, the universe beyond boundaries. That universe can be known but not known about. This means that the final state of consciousness passes beyond myth. It cannot be spoken about. The mystics universally testify to this as a fact of their experience. We can know that ultimate state but not say it or think it. The Tao that can be spoken is not the Tao. Christ-consciousness is direct, immediate, and nonverbal. In principle, no description, names, forms, words, or thoughts can be applied to this realm of consciousness. It is quite literally boundless.

The teachings of Jesus, particularly his two commandments, seem to imply this boundless, all-encompassing Christ-consciousness. "You shall love the Lord your God with all your heart, and with all your soul, and with all your mind" (Matt. 22:37), and "You shall love your neighbor as yourself" (Matt. 22:39). God is clearly the all-inclusive, all-loving one. Further, if we use the medieval description of God as a circle whose center is everywhere and whose circumference is nowhere, to love God means to have one's center everywhere and thus to have boundless love, an identity with all things. His second command means the same thing: to Jesus, neighbor was an all-inclusive, boundless term.

The teachings of Jesus have been used only a little in this work because the focus has been the outline of the mythic Hero story. Even there, a skeleton has been abstracted from the dynamic and lively tale, which is the story itself. One additional way of measuring the value of the insights I have offered is to compare them with the insights of Jesus' own teaching. For example, read the Beatitudes, interpreting them as a guide to the ascension of consciousness on the Hero's path to uniting Christ-consciousness.

This Christ-consciousness is in principle ineffable. The mystical tradition consistently affirms that Christ-consciousness can only be experienced, that one must "follow the way" to find it for oneself; then, however, one shall know immediately. The mystic says very simply,

> "Look inside. Deep inside. For the real self lies within." Now the mystic is not *describing* the real self as *being inside* you—he is *pointing* inside you. He is indeed saying to look within, not because the final answer actually resides within you and not without, but because as you carefully and consistently look inside, you sooner or later find outside. You realize, in other words, that the inside and the outside, the subject and the object, the seer and the seen are one, and thus you spontaneously fall into your natural state.[21]

▼

Notes

▼

ABBREVIATION:

CW   *The Collected Works of C. G. Jung*, 20 vols., ed. Gerhard
         Adler, Michael Fordham, Sir Herbert Read, and William
         McGuire; trans. R. F. C. Hull, Bollingen Series XX
         (Princeton: Princeton University Press, 1953–78). The
         following volumes are cited:
        5: *Symbols of Transformation* (1969)
        6: *Psychological Types* (1971)
        8: *The Structure and Dynamics of the Psyche* (1969)
  9, pt. 1: *The Archetypes and the Collective Unconscious* (1968)
  9, pt. 2: *Aion*(1959)
        11: *Psychology and Religion: West and East* (1958)
        13: *Alchemical Studies* (1967)
        17: *The Development of Personality* (1964)

Preface

1. James Yandell, *The Imitation of Jung: An Exploration of the Meaning of Jungian* (St. Louis, MO: Centerpoint Foundation, n.d.), pp. 36–37.

Introduction

1. Gary Zukav, *The Dancing Wu Li Masters: An Overview of the New Physics* (New York: Bantam, 1980), p. 92.

I. *The Mysterious Psyche: Mythic and Rational*

1. Joseph Campbell, *The Masks of God: Creative Mythology* (New York: Viking, 1968), pp. 4, 5, 6.
2. Henry James (ed.), *The Letters of William James*, 2 vols. (Boston: Atlantic Monthly, 1920), 1:225.
3. Theodore Roszak, *Where the Wasteland Ends* (Garden City, NY: Doubleday, Anchor, 1973), p. xxiv.
4. Carlos Castaneda, *Journey to Ixtlan* (New York: Simon & Schuster, 1972), pp.8–9.
5. Pitirim A. Sorokin, *The Crisis of Our Age* (New York: Dutton, 1945).
6. Alfred North Whitehead, *Science and the Modern World* (New York: Macmillan, 1953; rpt. New York: Free, 1967), p.12.

7. *CW* 6: 474, par. 814.
8. Paul Tillich, *The Dynamics of Faith* (New York: Harper & Row, 1957), pp. 41, 42, 43.
9. *CW* 6:475, par. 817.
10. Tillich, *Dynamics of Faith*, p. 43.
11. For further development, see, *CW* 6:ch. 11, "Definitions," under "Symbol"; 5:ch. 2, "Two Kinds of Thinking"; and 8:ch. 2, "The Transcendant Function."
12. Ernst Cassirer, *Language and Myth* (New York: Dover, 1946), p. 8.
13. Tillich, *Dynamics of Faith*, p. 45.
14. See Peter Berger and Thomas Luckmann, *The Social Construction of Reality*, (Garden City, NY: Doubleday, Anchor, 1967).

II: *The Transformation Key*

1. Ian G. Barbour, *Myths, Models and Paradigms* (New York: Harper & Row, 1974; rpt. 1976).

III: *Myth, Faith, and Symbols*

1. Marie-Louise von Franz, *Patterns of Creativity Mirrored in Creation Myths* (Zurich: The Analytical Psychology Club of New York, Inc., 1972), p. 9.
2. Ibid., pp. 9–10.
3. *CW* 8:42ff., par. 82ff.
4. *CW* 5:231, par. 344.
5. Erich Neumann, *The Origins and History of Consciousness* (Princeton: Princeton University, 1954; rpt. 1970), p. xvi.
6. *CW* 8:59, par. 111.
7. Joseph Campbell, *The Hero with a Thousand Faces* (Princeton: Princeton University, 1968), p. 18.

IV: *The Centrality of the Hero*

1. Campbell, *Hero*, p. 3.
2. William Irwin Thompson, *The Time Falling Bodies Take to Light* (New York: St. Martin's, 1981), p. 62.
3. June Singer, *Androgyny* (Garden City, NY: Anchor, Doubleday, 1976), p. 68.
4. Neumann, *Origins*, p. xvi. See also the works of Jean Piaget and Claude Lévi-Strauss.
5. Neumann, *Origins*, p. xx.
6. Ibid.
7. See Neumann, *Origins* and Campbell, *Hero*.
8. Neumann, *Origins*, p. 131.

V: *The Hero's Birth Story*

1. M. D. Goulder and M. L. Sanderson, "St. Luke's Genesis," *Journal of Theological Studies*, n.s., 8, pt. 1 (April 1957), pp. 12–30.
2. Neumann, *Origins*, p. 133
3. It is unfortunate, even tragic, that *darkness, black, blackness*, and *night* have such negative connotations, particularly as applied to persons whose skin is dark. This negativity seems to arise from the fact that every symbol system is based upon opposites. Studies of creation myths worldwide show the coming of light into a world of darkness as good. Symbolically, the light means the beginning of consciousness. Because of this fundamental opposition, a whole system of binary and contradictory aspects, which mark the ceaseless alternations of life and death, light and darkness, and other continuing cycles that make possible the dynamic nature of the world, has come into the perception/creation of reality.

   Black has a long association with death, gloom, evil, and, of course, night. In general, negative values historically have been associated with darkness, even in today's aesthetics and literature, e.g., Darth Vader in *Star Wars*. J. E. Cirlot, in his highly regarded book, *A Dictionary of Symbols* (New York: Philosophical Library, 1962), pp. 54–55, notes that the antithesis of black and white as symbols of the negative and positive are of the utmost importance. He cites many examples, including the colors of the two sphinxes in the Tarot pack and the opposition of the two worlds depicted in Indo-Aryan mythology as a black and white horse.

   Jung seemed to be somewhat prejudiced in his views of black people, often associating them with characteristics that are considered negative; yet, he was usually clear that our inner negativities and our outward prejudices are matters that need careful and loving attention. In this regard, note the symbolism of medieval Christian art: black stands for penitence, white for purity, but another axis of color cuts across these, i.e., red/gold. Red stands for charity and love. The Christian teaching says that love leads us out of the dichotomy. Jesus taught "love your enemy," certainly meaning the enemy within as well as without. In Christian art a new symbolism of white/red arose to signify this transcendence, and in alchemy this color scheme stands for the conjunction of opposites.

   Finally, "black is beautiful" indeed! Nowhere is this beauty so extolled and appreciated as in Charles Peguy's poem, "Night." He reveals in lovely imagery the soft and soothing quality of darkness, its sheer beauty and its utterly accepting nature. Black as the color of earth, the feminine, and the unconscious realm is negative only when viewed from the standpoint of an exclusive consciousness, a patriarchal modality, or the rationalistic myth. The red love for the night, as in Peguy's poem, restores the bridge and makes possible the higher synthesis of black and white symbolized in the Sacred Marriage and in the alchemical gold.

4. Charles Hartshorne and William Reese, *Philosophers Speak of God* (Chicago: University of Chicago, 1953), p. 2.

5. An example of a mythic account featuring a dragon is The Revelation to John, ch. 12. A full treatment of the Great Mother may be found in Erich Neumann, *The Great Mother* (Princeton: Princeton University, 1972).

6. Again, I express my indebtedness to Goulder and Sanderson, "St. Luke's Genesis," for many insights into Jesus' birth story.

7. *CW* 9, pt. 2:90, 92, pars. 147, 148.

VI: *The Meaning of the Birth of the Hero*

1. Neumann, *Great Mother*, p. 148.

2. *CW* 9, pt. 1:279, par. 498.

3. *CW* 5:271, par. 415.

4. Alfred North Whitehead, *Symbolism, Its Meaning and Effect* (New York: Macmillan, 1927; rpt., Capricorn, 1959), pp. 66, 69.

5. Ibid., pp. 69, 88.

6. C. G. Jung and C. Kerényi, *Essays on a Science of Mythology* (New York: Harper & Row, Harper Torchbooks, 1949), p. 85.

7. *CW* 5:355–56, par. 553.

8. Ibid., p. 374, par. 580.

9. *CW* 17:175, par. 298.

10. Ann B. Ulanov, *The Feminine: In Jungian Psychology and Christian Theology* (Evanston, IL: Northwestern University, 1971), p. 157.

VII: *Departure and Initiation*

1. Campbell, *Hero*, p. 51.

2. Ulanov, *The Feminine*, p. 33.

3. Cf. also Romans, ch. 6.

4. *CW* 5:321, par. 494.

5. Cirlot, *Dictionary of Symbols*, p. 365.

6. Neumann, *Great Mother*, pp. 59, 62.

7. Ibid., pp. 291f.

8. *CW* 5:293, par. 449.

9. Ibid., p. 330, par. 510.

10. Ibid., p. 337, par. 523.

11. Neumann, *Origins*, pp. 136, 148.

12. Neumann, *Great Mother*, p. 33.

13. Erich Neumann, *Depth Psychology and a New Ethic* (New York: Harper & Row, Harper Torchbooks, 1973), p. 137.

14. *CW* 11:196, par. 290.
15. Neumann, *Depth Psychology*, p. 143.
16. Ibid.
17. Ibid., p. 123.
18. Quoted in Roland Bainton, *Here I Stand* (New York: Abingdon-Cokesbury, 1950), p. 82.

VIII: *The Battle with the Dragon*

1. *CW* 5:230, par. 341.
2. Ibid., 231, par. 342.
3. Campbell, *Hero*, p. 15.
4. Martin Noth, *The History of Israel* (New York: Harper, 1958), p. 332.
5. Campbell, *Hero*, p. 347.
6. There is a fine discussion of this point in Campbell, *Hero*, pp. 155ff.
7. *CW* 5:232, par. 345.
8. Dorothy M. Slusser and Gerald H. Slusser, *The Jesus of Mark's Gospel* (Philadelphia: Westminster, 1967), p. 37.
9. Ibid., pp. 40–41.
10. Neumann, *Origins*, pp. 172–73.
11. Ibid., p. 174.
12. Ibid., p. 176.
13. Ibid., p. 184. See the opening paragraphs of this chapter for discussion of this analysis of archetypal symbols.
14. Ibid., p. 187.
15. Ibid.
16. Ibid., pp. 189–90. The parallel with the elder brother in Jesus' parable of the prodigal son is clear.
17. Cf. Acts 2:17ff. and Joel 2:28ff.
18. Slusser and Slusser, *Jesus of Mark's Gospel*, pp. 127–28.
19. Erich Neumann, *The Child* (New York: Putnam, 1973), p. 43.

IX: *The Sacred Marriage of the Hero*

1. Singer, *Androgyny*, p. 332.
2. Frances Wickes, *The Inner World of Choice* (Englewood Cliffs, NJ: Prentice-Hall, 1963), p. 162.
3. Neumann, *Origins*, p. 213.
4. Campbell, *Hero*, pp. 249–51.
5. Singer, *Androgyny*, p. 169.
6. Neumann, *Origins*, pp. 205–6.
7. Ibid., p. 182.
8. Ibid., pp. 186ff.
9. Joseph Campbell, *The Masks of God: Primitive Mythology* (New York: Viking, 1970), pp. 170–71.
10. Ibid., pp. 179–80.

11. Mircea Eliade, *Myths, Dreams and Mysteries*, (New York: Harper, 1960), pp. 183–84.
12. Mircea Eliade, *Patterns in Comparative Religions* (New York: New American Library, 1974), pp. 360–61.
13. Cirlot, *Dictionary*, pp. 89, 182.
14. Natalie Curtis, *The Indians' Book*, (New York: Harper, 1907), pp. 38–39.
15. Campbell, *Masks: Primitive Mythology*, p. 253.
16. Ibid., p. 311.
17. Eliade, *Comparative Religions*, pp. 283ff.
18. Ibid., p. 293.
19. Campbell, *Masks: Primitive Mythology*, p. 120–21.
20. *CW* 13:317–18, par. 418.
21. Cirlot, *Dictionary*, p. 99.
22. *CW* 13:333, par. 448.
23. Mircea Eliade, *Shamanism* (Princeton: Princeton University, 1964), p. 265.
24. Ibid.
25. Campbell, *Masks: Primitive Mythology*, pp. 414ff.
26. Joseph L. Henderson and Maud Oakes, *The Wisdom of the Serpent* (New York: George Braziller, 1963), p.24.
27. Cirlot. *Dictionary*, pp. 345, 346.
28. Neumann, *Origins*, pp. 220–21.
29. See ibid., p. 221.
30. Ibid., pp. 226, 227.
31. Ibid., pp. 244, 246.
32. Ibid., p. 249.
33. Ibid., p. 255.
34. Ibid., p. 415.
35. St. Augustine, *Sermo Suppositus*, quoted in *CW* 5:269, n. 152.
36. Heinrich Zimmer, "Death and Rebirth in the Light of India," *Man and Transformation*, ed. Joseph Campbell (New York: Pantheon, 1964), pp. 343, 347.

X: *Summary and Conclusions*

1. Neumann, *Origins*, p. 131.
2. Ibid., p. 263.
3. Ibid., p. 301.
4. Whitehead, *Symbolism*, p. 69.
5. Neumann, *Origins*, p. 174.
6. Zukav, *Dancing Wu Li Masters*, p. 92.
7. Ibid., p. 200.
8. Helen Luke, *Dark Wood to White Rose: A Study of Meanings in Dante's Divine Comedy*, (Pecos, NM: Dove, 1975), p. 86.

9. *CW* 9 pt. 2:165, par. 253.

10. Aldous Huxley, Introduction to *The Song of God: Bhagavad-Gita*, trans. Swami Prabhavanada and Christopher Isherwood (New York: Mentor, 1946), p. 13.

11. Quoted in Ken Wilber, *Up from Eden* (Garden City, NY: Doubleday, 1981), p. 6.

12. Ibid., p. 4.

13. Ibid., p. 3.

14. Ken Wilber, *No Boundary* (Boulder, CO: Shambhala, 1981), p. 24.

15. Ken Wilber, *The Atman Project*, (Wheaton, IL: Theosophical, 1980), pp. 102, 104–7.

16. Wilber, *Up from Eden*, p. 12.

17. Ibid., p. 13.

18. Ibid.

19. Ibid., pp. 14–15.

20. Wilber, *No Boundary*, p. 38.

21. Ibid., p. 56.

Index

Orthodoxy, 30
Orwell, George, 150
Osiris, 76, 121, 124–126, 139

Palestine, 115
Palm Sunday, 96, 101–104
Parables of Jesus, 23, 106–108,
    140
Participation mystique, 39, 134,
    138
Passover, 105, 108–109
Patterns
  of culture, 59
  death of, 60–61
  of energy, 16
  physiological, 10–11, 25
  of symbols, 34
Paul, 45, 53, 65, 126, 144
Perennial Philosophy, 147
Peter, 78, 120
Phaeton, 75
Piaget, Jean, 36
Pilate, 114, 118
Pilgrimage. See Journey
Pisces, 55
Planter, mythology of the,
    109–114, 120, 126
Polarities, 15, 51, 61, 63, 116,
    132
Positivism, 13, 14, 30, 62, 129,
    148
Prodigal son, 140
Projection, 36–39
  and contrasexual aspect, 142
  destructiveness of, 85, 128
  and Rorschach test, 134
  and Shadow, 65, 87
Prometheus, 154
Protestants, 85
Psyche, 4–5, 23–24, 132–133
  alienation, 105
  and ego, 21, 108
  and Hero, 42–43, 46–49
  and inner conflict, 68–69

integration of the, 74–75, 144
and language, 18
products of the, 6–7
and projection, 65
and renewal, 124
and Self, 34, 39
universal structure of the, 33,
    45–46, 130
Psychological Approach to the
    Trinity, A, 76
Psychology, 1, 5, 31
Psychopomp, 77

Quantum theory, 15, 131
Queen of Heaven, 121
Queen of the Underworld, 121

Rank, Otto, 92
Rationalism, 12–13
  and ego, 26, 149
  as view of reality, 8, 14–15, 131,
    141, 148
Reality, 9–10, 19, 20
Rebirth. See Transformation
Reformation, 85
Relativity, 14–15, 131
Religion, 16–17, 41–42, 131
Resurrection, 112–113, 122, 126,
    127, 144–145
Revelation, 7, 41, 44, 69
Riesman, David, 134
Rituals, 7, 39, 43
Roman Catholic Church, 85
Romanticism, 14
Rorschach test, 38, 134
Roszak, Theodore, 9
Russia, 84, 85, 87
Ruth, 42, 74, 95

Sacrifice, 110–111
Salvation, 22, 69
Samson, 54
Samuel, 54
Sanctification, 150
Sapientia, 117